Competitive
WEIGHTLIFTING

By R. V. FODOR

STERLING PUBLISHING CO., INC.   NEW YORK
Oak Tree Press Co., Ltd.   London & Sydney

Dedication

To the Albuquerque lifters—especially Doug, Jed, and Butch

Acknowledgments

The author and publishers wish to thank the Amateur Athletic Union for their kind permission to refer to their rules and regulations for weightlifting. Special thanks are due Jed Harris who contributed greatly to the accuracy of the chapter on Olympic lifting.

Anatomical drawings from "Bridgman's Complete Guide to Drawing from Life" © Sterling Publishing Co., Inc., New York

Photo Credits

Photograph of Vasili Alexeev by Bruce H. Klemens. All other photographs by the author.

Contents

SECTION I

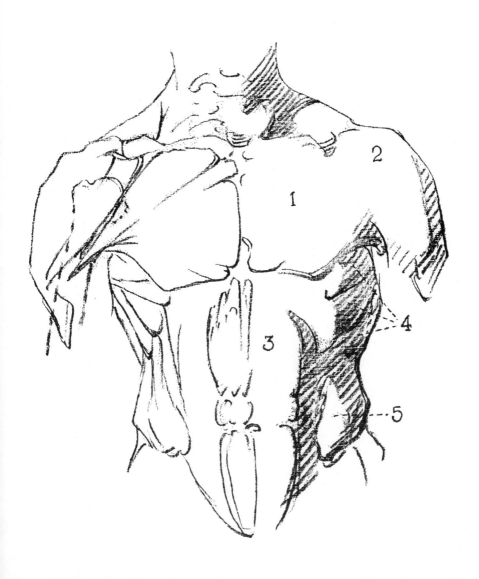

What's Weightlifting All About?

In July, 1976, during the XXI Olympiad in Montreal, Quebec, Canada, Vasili Alexeev of the Soviet Union jerked a 562-lb. (255-kg.) barbell over his head. That feat represented the most weight any man had ever lifted and held over his head and it easily helped Alexeev win an Olympic gold medal in the super-heavyweight class. For the second consecutive Olympiad, Alexeev had earned the title of the world's strongest man. His adeptness with a barbell, often loaded with more than a quarter ton of iron plates, has made Alexeev a national hero in the Soviet Union and, in fact, helped him at one time to be elected the Soviet athlete of the year.

But Alexeev has achieved more with his weightlifting than domestic and personal fame. His super strength has in recent years given a super lift to the world of competitive weightlifting. His remarkable feats on the lifting platform are known to the average sports fan, and this, in turn, has given further recognition and popularity to the relatively "small" sport of weightlifting.

Yes, weightlifting is indeed a sport, and a highly competitive international sport at that. Furthermore, it is a sport that claims some of the most physically fit, well co-ordinated, and well developed athletes in the entire sports world—not to mention some of the oldest (weightlifters frequently do not "peak out" until they are in their thirties).

The sport of weightlifting has only recently been gaining greater recognition in America and other English-speaking countries, after many years of being considered simply a means of training and conditioning for other competitive sports. Currently, there are almost 10,000 people registered in the United States as amateur athletes who compete in weightlifting—and that number grows each year. Every month, dozens of Amateur Athletic Union-sanctioned meets are held at various locations throughout the

Illus. 1—Vasili Alexeev sets the world record for the clean and jerk.

United States, and international contests are held weekly in over fifty countries of the world. In the English-speaking countries alone, there are hundreds of men (and women these days, too) participating in weightlifting meets, competing for trophies and recognition as athletes.

Despite the increasing popularity of weightlifting and the boost that weightlifting receives from coverage of the Olympics and the exceptional lifters like Alexeev, there are still not enough opportunities for the uninitiated to learn what the competition is all about or how to prepare for it. What exactly are the lifts performed? How is the competition scored and judged? What are the physical, age, and bodyweight prerequisites? What are the training techniques? Indeed, many of the world's millions of sports enthusiasts fail to realize that there are two types of competitive weightlifting events recognized internationally: *Olympic lifting* and *powerlifting*.

While dozens of books are available on other competitive sports that describe the proper techniques, rules and regulations, and conditioning procedures, there is a paucity of information about competitive weight-lifting. That's what this book is about and that's the gap this book fills! It is intended to introduce the uninitiated to all aspects of competitive weightlifting, as well as to offer the conditioning and training techniques necessary to turn any man or woman into a competitive Olympic or power weightlifter. In addition, I hope that this book helps bring even further popularity to weightlifting, encouragement for greater participation and funding, and the respect and attention that it deserves as a competitive sport and for the athletes who compete in it.

Weightlifting Today

For the past thirty years, the use of barbells, dumbbells, and weights has been as common during adolescence as swimming, bicycling, and basketball. Nearly every young male has lifted weights at one time or another—either with the hope of seeing a rapid change in his physique and stamina, or with the idea of improving his ability in some strength-related sport. However, few who start with weights stay with a regular training routine for more than a year, usually from a lack of patience. Pronounced physical improvements from weightlifting do not come overnight and many who start a routine want quick, tangible results. On the other hand, many athletes who start on a weight-training regimen and who have the discipline to stay with it, not only see a desired improvement in all-around physical fitness and health, but find they are gradually caught up in a competitive atmosphere. They become the competitive weightlifters!

Certainly there are dozens of ways to lift, pull, and push a barbell, but what does competitive weightlifting consist of? How is one's strength, co-ordination, and athletic skill judged during competition? How do you get deeply enough involved in the sport to compete? To answer these questions, it is first necessary to divide lifting competition into its respective categories—Olympic lifting and powerlifting.

Olympic Lifting

Today there are only two official Olympic-style lifts: the snatch and the clean and jerk. These lifts demand not only overall body strength and flexibility, but great athletic co-ordination and finesse. These lifts are discussed in detail on pages 56–75, but they are briefly described here as an introduction.

The *snatch* is a lift in which a barbell is brought in *one continuous movement* from the floor to a position over the lifter's head with outstretched arms. Although the lifter falls into a squat position midway through the lift, the final position for the snatch is an erect stance.

In contrast, the lift known as the *clean and jerk* is a two-movement lift. The barbell is first brought from the floor to the chest of the lifter as he achieves an erect stance with the weight. That movement is called the "clean." After a momentary pause, the barbell is pushed (or jerked) upwards and the lift is completed with the competitor holding the barbell overhead with outstretched arms.

Until 1972, a third lift, called a *press,* was also used in competition. The press, which is still a popular exercise used in training, consists of cleaning the weight and then gradually pushing (not jerking) the barbell directly overhead. It was omitted from competition, however, because of the extreme difficulty referees had in judging correct performance. (Competitors would tend to bend over backwards while pressing, bringing in too much of the chest muscles to assist the shoulders and arms.)

Like boxers or wrestlers, Olympic lifters are classified into different groups on the basis of their bodyweight, competing with other individuals of similar physical stature. There are ten weight categories, ranging from flyweights at 114½ lb. (52 kg.) and less, to super-heavyweights at 242½ lb. (110 kg.) and heavier. Naturally, the amount of weight an individual is able to lift is directly related to his or her bodyweight and size.

Respectable barbell poundages (considered heavy enough to qualify an Olympic-style competitor as "good") are snatches of 175–200 lb. (80–90 kg.) for a man of 150 lb. (68 kg.) bodyweight, and snatches of 250–300 lb. (110–135 kg.) for a 200-lb. (90-kg.) man. Clean and jerks of 225–250 lb. (100–110 kg.) and 300–350 lb. (135–160 kg.) are quite good for a 150-lb. (68-kg.) man and 200-lb. (90-kg.) man, respectively. These poundages are far from world-record lifts, but don't be discouraged if they seem very heavy to you. Obviously, all lifters started with "light" weights, and the ability of an individual to reach "respectable" poundages is largely a function of personal determination and dedication to training (as it is in any sport). It takes time, patience, desire, and hard work.

Powerlifting

Powerlifting requires much more in the way of brute strength from the lifter than athletic co-ordination and flexibility. There are now three powerlifts: the squat, the bench press, the deadlift. These will, of course,

Illus. 2—Serious powerlifting requires great strength, but anyone can do it for exercise and fun.

be discussed in detail later, but as an introduction, the following descriptions are presented.

The *squat* is a deep knee bend accomplished with a barbell perched across the back of the lifter's shoulders. The object of the lift is to squat down with the barbell (no problem there) until the tops of the thighs are parallel to the floor. The lifter then tries to return to his original erect stance with the barbell still across his shoulders.

A *bench press* is performed while in a horizontal position on a bench. The lifter picks a loaded barbell from a rack located above his head and holds it momentarily above his chest with straight arms. He then lowers the bar to his chest and presses it up again until his arms are fully extended.

The *deadlift* is the simplest of the powerlifts and it requires the least amount of athletic skill. It does, however, call for a great deal of strength in the back and legs. The lifter merely grasps the barbell and pulls it off the floor until he reaches a final position in an erect stance with the hips locked, shoulders thrust backwards, and the arms extended down, holding the barbell against the fronts of the thighs. The deadlift is a simple test which determines the maximum weight a person can actually get off the floor. In many cases this is well over a quarter of a ton.

The following poundages would probably place a contestant rather high in a powerlifting competition: for a 150-lb. (68-kg.) man, a squat of

350 lb. (160 kg.), a bench press of 265 lb. (120 kg.), and a deadlift of 450 lb. (200 kg.); for a 200-lb. (90-kg.) man, a squat of 450 lb. (200 kg.), a bench press of 325 lb. (150 kg.), and a deadlift of 550 lb. (250 kg.) would stand up well during a meet and perhaps earn a trophy.

Powerlifters, like Olympic lifters, compete within 10 weight divisions. The inclusion of light bodyweight classes, such as the flyweight and featherweight classes, allows small men to excel in their own right. For many sports, great height or bodyweight is essential to becoming a skilled competitor. This is not so in competitive weightlifting.

History of the Sport

Weightlifting as a competitive sport was introduced as an international event at the first modern Olympics in Athens, Greece, in 1896. Participants there were mainly European, and interest in the sport remained concentrated in Europe for the following 25 years.

In the United States, the first contest of any significance was held in 1926 at the Sesquicentennial celebration in Philadelphia. Because it was a relatively new sport at the time, the participants were not well-trained and the weights lifted in competition do not compare at all with the high poundages lifted by today's athletes. For example, the best snatches during the late 1920's by a 150-lb. (68-kg.) man were only about 170 lb. (77 kg.), and a respectable clean and jerk by a 200-lb. (90-kg.) lifter was less than 300 lb. (135 kg.). These weights are far less than many local records that hold today. In these early days, competition was divided among five different lifts: the one-hand snatch, one-hand clean and jerk, two-hands military press, two-hands snatch, and the two-hands clean and jerk. Weightlifters had to marshal their concentration, strength and endurance throughout a long contest. With the emphasis today on only two lifts, competitors have been able to concentrate their training techniques and systems, which has resulted in dramatic gains in the poundages lifted.

In the U.S., the Amateur Athletic Union began to sanction contests in 1929, and an AAU-recognized team performed at the 1932 Olympics held in the Los Angeles Coliseum. The U.S. lifters found, however, that they were no match for the well-trained foreign lifters, long accustomed to tough international competition. It was obvious that there was really no way for the quality of the lifting in the U.S. to go but up. Throughout the 1930's and on through the 40's and 50's, United States' weightlifters improved until they had become supreme in world competition. However, much of this improvement came during the 1940's, when European lifters were understandably preoccupied with the Second World War.

Illus. 3—The deadlift involves pulling the most possible weight off the floor.

Since the early 1960's, advanced training regimens in eastern European countries have propelled their athletes to world domination in many sporting activities, such as swimming, track and field, and weightlifting. For the most part, the top international weightlifting competition today is largely between the athletes of the Soviet Union, Bulgaria, East Germany, Rumania, and Poland. In all of these countries, Olympic-style weightlifting is a highly-respected sport and followed by a substantial portion of the sports-minded community.

The story of powerlifting is different. Although the three powerlifts have been performed by athletes for years as strength exercises, it was only in the early 1960's that actual powerlifting contests began. During those initial years, activity in powerlifting was almost entirely restricted to the United States. The true birth of powerlifting did not come until 1965 when the AAU first recognized and sanctioned it as a sport. Since that time, powerlifting has grown at a much greater rate than Olympic lifting.

In 1971, the first international powerlifting contest was held in Harrisburg, Pennsylvania. Although it did not attract as wide a range of athletes as an Olympic-style meet, it marked a decisive step in the growth of the sport. In the years following the first international contest, participants in international powerlifting competitions have come mainly from English-speaking countries. Although 28 countries now belong to the International Powerlifting Federation (over 50 countries recognize Olympic-style lifting as a competitive sport), usually no more than 10 or 12 countries are represented at any particular meet.

There have been several prominent individual supporters of competitive weightlifting in the United States and Great Britain. First among these, virtually since weightlifting's inception as a competitive sport, has been the octogenerian, Bob Hoffman, of York, Pennsylvania. Hoffman started as a manufacturer of weightlifting equipment, and over the years, increased his committment until he became a champion himself and eventually an Olympic coach. Hoffman has coached lifters at the Olympic games for three decades and has done more to promote weightlifting in the United States than any other individual.

Weightlifting is not without periodical literature. *Strength and Health* emphasizes Olympic lifting, and *Muscular Development* caters to power-lifters. *Iron Man* magazine serves up an equal balance of Olympic lifting, powerlifting, plus bodybuilding, a sport not discussed in this book, in which weightlifting is used to develop outstanding physiques. In Great Britain, *The Strength Athlete* covers both Olympic and powerlifting and in Australia, *Powerlifting* is available.

SECTION II

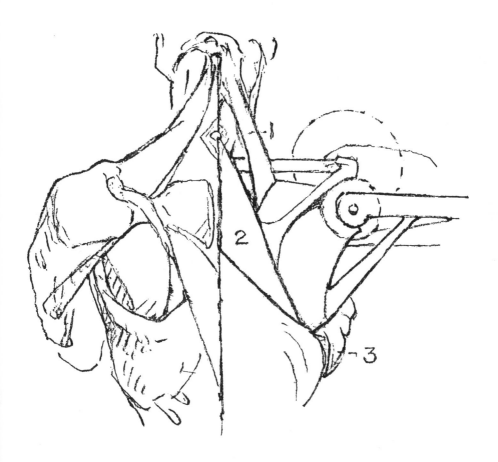

Illus. 4

How to Get Started

The primary objective of this book is to prepare you for weightlifting competition. Regardless of background and experience, even regardless of age, anyone can get started in weightlifting. All you need are three to four hours per week, access to weights, and the ambition and desire to become physically fit and a competitor in a fascinating sport.

Where to Begin

Unlike other sports, you can start a conditioning course for weightlifting right in your home. All you need is a set of weights consisting of enough bars and plates to construct a barbell and two dumbbells for a total of approximately 100 lb. (45 kg.). You can buy new weights at most department stores or sporting-goods shops, or you can order them from companies that advertise in weightlifting magazines. But there's no reason to begin with brand-new equipment. Quality weights do not wear out. More economical sources of good quality weights may be found by leafing through the classified-ad section of your newspaper. As with any other special interest, there are always people who have invested money in weightlifting and found later that it was not the activity for them.

It is necessary to point out that this home equipment is only for breaking into weightlifting and for the relatively light conditioning and exercising

Illus. 5—Weightlifting need not be expensive. Shown here is a set of weights purchased at three garage sales.

period that follows. For actual competitive weightlifting and for serious training, special "Olympic" equipment is used, which consists of a larger bar with weight-plates up to 45 lb. (25 kg.). This equipment, which is too large and cumbersome to bring into most homes, can be found at most gymnasiums. (Its use is discussed on pages 123–124.) After an initial period of diligent home training, you will soon outgrow your home weights and have to move up to an "Olympic" set.

When planning to lift weights at home, you may wish to consider using weight-plates that are vinyl covered. Vinyl-covered plates are usually concrete discs covered with plastic. These weights are quiet to use but, unfortunately, are not as sturdy or long-lasting as iron plates.

The advantage of breaking into weightlifting at home is that you have the privacy and freedom to work out at any time of day you choose. However, do not overlook the advantages of gymnasiums, which offer an environment where others are lifting as well (many of whom may be beginners). You may find that the athletic environment at a YWCA or YMCA, filled with physical-fitness enthusiasts, increases your motivation and is well worth the nominal membership fee.

If you are a student, look into the weightlifting facilities available at your school. Generally, university gymnasiums have enough weightlifting equipment to accommodate both the beginner and the advanced lifter. Well-equipped weight rooms will have not only barbells and dumbbells, but are also stocked with special pushing, pulling, and cable apparatus called Universal Gyms®, which can be used to augment your weight-lifting and training regimen.

On the other hand, gym-and-swim health clubs and spas are not what you really need if you have serious competitive weightlifting in mind. These facilities are geared more for the bodybuilder and not for the individual who hopes to maximize his or her strength and athletic ability. In addition, membership fees can become uncomfortably high.

Finally, check in your area to see if there are any clubs or gyms devoted entirely to weightlifting.

Weightlifting Terms

There is really not much in the way of special terminology for the novice to understand and use properly. *Rep,* for repetition, *set, spotter,* and *pump* are all that you need to know to fit right in with those already involved in the "iron game."

Reps tell you the number of consecutive times a particular exercise is

Illus. 6—Always have one or more spotters on hand when performing a heavy lift.

performed. For example, if you pick up a barbell and press it over your head 5 times before placing it down, you have done 5 reps. You have also completed one set of presses. A *set* is any group of repetitions. You will often do 5 sets of a particular exercise, with 8 to 10 reps per set.

A *spotter* is another lifter who carefully observes you perform a set for safety purposes. Most exercises do not warrant a spotter, particularly if you can easily and safely drop the weights out of your hands. But for some movements with a barbell, such as squats or bench presses, where you may extend yourself slightly beyond your limit, it is essential to have one or more assistants to *spot* you and to help remove the barbell if you are unable to hold it or control it.

During intense exercise of particular muscles, blood rushes to that muscle area to provide necessary oxygen and to flush away any toxic material. The term *pump* refers to this flooding of muscles with blood after some type of resistance exercise. Usually, that "pumped-up" feeling lasts about an hour. Recently, the phrase "pumping iron" has become popular and was coined in reference to using weights (iron) to work individual muscle groups so intensively that they swell with blood. You will immediately know what a pump is after doing a few intensive sets of an arm exercise.

Starting from Scratch

Before you begin to lift heavy weights in competition, you must gradually condition your body so that it can handle hard training. This section will show you how to condition your body for serious weightlifting. Your first goal is to get into condition and establish a solid foundation to build on. This is the same process that athletes go through for most other sports. No one, for example, could hope to run in a 10,000-metre race without having first conditioned his body to endure distance running.

Getting into shape requires you to perform a series of special exercises to tone up all the major muscle groups. Later, when you are ready to specialize in the competitive lifts, you will concentrate on particular supplementary exercises and will not have to continue with all of the movements you selected for toning up. You will give your attention only to those exercises that are directly applicable to the lifts in which you want to achieve proficiency.

Dress appropriately any time you work out. Wear a sweatshirt or a complete sweatsuit. If you opt for shorts in warm weather, be sure that they are not confining and are made from material that stretches when you are in bending or stooping positions.

Be careful about staying warm during a workout. In cold weather, be sure your workout area is adequately heated and that you are dressed warmly. In warm weather, stay out of air currents and away from blasting air conditioners. Always wear at least a tee-shirt to absorb perspiration.

Wear quality athletic shoes, not only to protect your feet, but to accustom yourself to working out in attire that is acceptable for competition. Also, for lifts requiring good balance, such as those with squatting and pressing movements, it is important to have arch supports in your shoes.

Illus. 7—The Universal Gym®️ is a versatile apparatus on which almost every body part can be exercised.

Beginners must approach their initial conditioning sensibly. Too often, they become over-ambitious, lifting 5 or 6 days a week, and several hours at a time. Keeping your body in a nearly continuous state of fatigue and with torn-down tissue will only defeat your purpose. You *must* allow your body adequate time to recover. On the other hand, you must stimulate your muscles enough so that they steadily respond and develop. Work out no more than a total of 3 to 4 hours per week during your initial break-in period and divide your workouts evenly between three alternate days, such as Monday, Wednesday, and Friday. In addition, most people should get anywhere from 7 to 9 hours of sleep each night. Adequate rest is essential for building strength. (The time of day when you work out is not critical, but try to be consistent in the time of day from one workout to the next.)

Begin each workout with a proper warm-up, which allows your respiratory and circulatory systems to adjust to the demand for oxygen that will come when you begin your actual workout. A warm-up also serves to loosen joints and ligaments and helps prevent the possibility of unnecessarily and painfully pulling or stretching a muscle. A thorough warm-up is a necessity for both beginning and experienced lifters. In fact, experienced Olympic lifters may spend 10 or 15 minutes or more going through a warm-up and stretching routine before practice or competition.

A 5-minute warm-up should be adequate for beginners starting on a conditioning course. Use the following as a basis for your warm-up exercises:

- 50 to 100 side bends
- 10 forward toe touches and 10 back bends
- 25 jumping jacks
- 10 deep knee bends
- 10 to 20 push-ups (press-ups)
- 1 minute of jogging in place
- 20 trunk rotations (twisting) with a bar

You certainly don't have to do all of these movements before a particular workout. Experiment with them and decide which leave you best prepared for the weightlifting routine you choose. A satisfactory warm-up should cause you to perspire a bit and leave you physically loose and energetic and mentally ready to get into your routine of weightlifting.

To achieve the full benefit from any lift, it is imperative that you perform each rep as it was intended to be. Use the correct form. Breathe properly. Work at a good pace. Choose the proper weight. Always move the weight through the maximum range of motion possible to ensure full contraction and extension of the muscles involved. Otherwise, you will be short-changing yourself. Also, don't bring into the movement body parts that

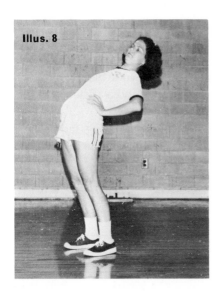

Illus. 8

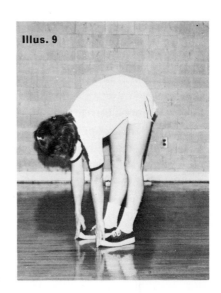

Illus. 9

Illus. 8-11—Always stretch muscles before lifting heavy weights. These exercises will help loosen almost all major muscle groups.

Illus. 10

Illus. 11

were not intended to assist in the lifting of the weight. For example, don't lean over backwards to assist curling a barbell with your biceps.

In general, you should always inhale during the least strenuous part of a movement and exhale during the actual strain. For example, if you are going to press a barbell over your head, exhale as you press it upwards and inhale as you lower it to your shoulders.

The pace you set for your workout and the time you rest between sets varies according to the individual. You must allow your body enough time to recover from the previous set so that you can perform the next exercise in good form. But don't overdo it. Long breaks let your body cool down and can lead to strains and other injuries. In general, breaks should be less than 2 minutes, but at least 15 seconds long.

What is the proper weight to use for each weightlifting movement? Simply put, that depends on your current strength. Experiment until you can comfortably perform a given movement at a particular rate in the range of 5 to 10 reps per set of exercises. No one can tell you how much weight to begin with. What seems like a ton to one beginner may feel like a sack of feathers to another.

One final word for those starting from scratch (or who have had a long layoff): expect some muscle soreness after the first few workouts. Fortunately, sore muscles do not last long, and will usually clear up after the first week of steady lifting. However, if soreness seems like it may be a concern, start at a particularly easy pace and with a light load during the first workout or two.

The best conditioning scheme is progressive, gradually accustoming your muscles to doing more and heavier work. During the first few weeks, you will note a rapid increase in strength, but probably not much in muscle size. Changes in body proportions come about more slowly than increases in strength.

Begin any new exercise with a weight light enough to allow your body to become accustomed to the movement. Do at least one or two sets of 5 to 10 reps with a weight substantially lighter than the weight you will later select for your workout. Ten is the maximum number of repetitions per set that you need to condition any part of the body. Therefore, for each exercise you select, base your starting poundage on a weight with which you can perform one set at 8 reps comfortably.

Plan to do three sets at each exercise at the chosen weight, and try over the next few workouts, to work up to as many as 10 reps for each set. It may not come easy at first, but set a goal of *adding one rep per set at each workout*. For example, say you can now do curls with a 50-lb. (25-kg.) barbell, the first set at 8 reps, the second set at 8 reps, and the third set at 7 reps. Try to get that up to 9, 9, and 8 reps at your next session. When you can perform 10 reps for two sets comfortably, add weight and start back at 8 reps for the first set. For the small muscle groups, like the arms, add 5 lb. (2.5 kg.). For the large muscle groups, like the legs and back, add 10 lb. (5 kg.).

Gradually increasing the weight and reps is the most sensible way to good conditioning and renewed strength, and it makes injuries and overworking virtually impossible. But it is also clear that you can only go so far with this type of regimen. When you reach a plateau, or "sticking point," for a certain exercise (which may not happen for several months of lifting) cut back on the number of reps and add weight. Then, once you can work the heavier weight for low reps, you should be able to drop down in weight and do the higher number of reps you were "sticking" at earlier. True strength is built by performing heavy "singles," or sets of one rep; but don't attempt great lifts until you have been into weightlifting for some time and feel that you have established a solid foundation.

Eventually, you will reach poundages in certain exercises for which 8 or 10 reps for 3 sets is just unreasonable. Don't hesitate to adjust your routine. Do more sets, up to 5, at lower reps, also about 5. Ultimately, you may reach a point when 5 reps will be your maximum number and you will find yourself doing several sets of double and triple reps as part of your regimen. By that time, you should be embarked on a regular training routine leading toward either Olympic lifting or powerlifting.

Strengthening the Legs

Nearly all competitive lifts require strong and well-conditioned legs. With proper use of a barbell and with the use of the leg-extension and leg-press machines found in most gymnasiums, you will have no problem preparing your legs for any lift.

Illus. 12a and b—Squats are great developers of leg muscles. Remember to keep your back straight.

Squats: This movement is one of the powerlifts and is described in great detail on pages 95–99. The squat is simply a deep knee bend, but complicated with the added resistance of a barbell resting behind your neck on your shoulders. Placing the bar on your back will require the use of squat racks or squat stands (which most gyms have) on which to set the bar before and after the exercise. Duck beneath the bar, lift it off the rack and onto your shoulders, and take a step away from the rack. Get set with your feet about shoulder-width apart and with a nearly erect stance (Illus. 12a). Take a deep breath and dip down, exhaling, until your thighs are parallel to the floor (Illus. 12b). Then, quickly rise out of the bottom position using the power in your legs. Rise up with an erect back, still exhaling, and with your head up. It is essential when squatting to keep your back as straight as possible and your head up.

3–5 sets; 5–10 reps

Front squats: This is a variation of the regular squat, and a great exercise for developing the tops of the thighs, the quadriceps. Hold the barbell at your upper chest just below your neck (Illus. 13a). Proceed to squat as before (Illus. 13b), and push up out of the squat with your legs. As with rear squats, begin with your lungs full, and then exhale during the entire movement. Be sure to keep your head up and your back straight.

3–5 sets; 5–10 reps

Illus. 13a and b—Squatting in this manner especially develops the quadriceps.

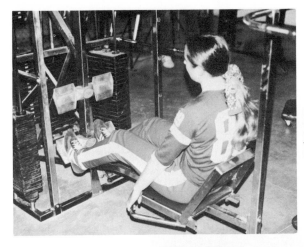

Illus. 14—Use the Universal Gym® for leg presses. Move the seat forward for maximum leg movement.

Illus. 15—The upper pedals provide less leverage and thus require more strength.

Leg presses: The special apparatus required for leg presses is part of the Universal Gym® and can be found at any well-equipped gymnasium. Leg presses are done in a sitting position by pressing pedals to lift a stack of weights (Illus. 14 and 15). Some machines have two sets of pedals. Use the lower set to work the thighs effectively. The lesser leverage on the upper pedals makes them more difficult to press. You can also vary the position of the seat. Maximum leg movement is accomplished by setting the seat into its most forward position.

3–5 sets; 5–10 reps

Leg curls: You can also use the leg-extension machine to strengthen the backs of your thighs, the hamstrings. Lie on your stomach and hook your ankles behind the top set of rollers (Illus. 16). Now, curl your legs back as far as possible, return, and repeat.

3–5 sets; 10 reps

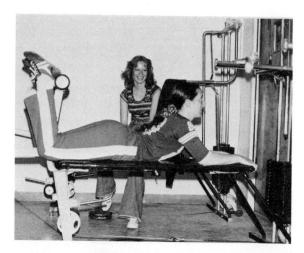

Illus. 16—Leg curls build up the hamstrings.

Illus. 17 (left)—The leg-extension machine allows you to condition the tops of the thighs. Illus. 18 (right)—This seemingly simple exercise will thoroughly work the calves.

Leg extensions: A leg-extension machine (also found in most gymnasiums) is a great apparatus for conditioning the upper thighs. Simply sit on the edge of the bench, lock your feet behind the lower set of rollers, and straighten your legs (Illus. 17). Lower your feet and repeat.

3–5 sets; 10 reps

Calf raises: Building calf strength is not particularly vital to good lifting, but if you want to leave no stone unturned, take a barbell and a thick block of wood and work on your calves. Start as you would for a squat with the barbell on your back. Place your toes on the block so that the heels of your feet hang off and are lower. Then, rise up and down on the balls of your feet (Illus. 18). It will not take too many reps to make your calves feel like they are on fire. In fact, you may want to begin this exercise by omitting the added weight of the barbell.

3–5 sets; 10–20 reps

Building Up the Back

Like the leg muscles, the back muscles play a major role in almost every competitive lift. The back is also a part of the body that gives many

Illus. 19a—The deadlift, also a competition powerlift, builds up the back and legs.

Illus. 19b—Remember to use one palm-up and one palm-down grip.

people great pain and discomfort. For that reason alone, it will pay you to build up your back and avoid future ailments.

Deadlifts : The deadlift is a great back exercise, working both the lower and upper portions of the back. It is one of the powerlifts described in detail on pages 103–106. The deadlift simply requires that you lift a barbell from the floor to your hips. Stand with your feet a little wider than the width of your shoulders and grasp the bar with one hand around the bar palm up and the other hand around and palm down (Illus. 19a). Bend down to get set, take a deep breath, and begin the pull. Initially, use driving leg force to raise the bar and exhale throughout the movement (Illus. 19b). Even by using your legs for much of the deadlift, your back will still get a good workout. Lower the bar and repeat.

3–5 sets; 5–10 reps

Illus. 20a—The stiff-legged deadlift isolates the back and does not involve the legs.

Illus. 20b—Start this exercise with a light weight until you're sure your back can take it.

Stiff-legged deadlifts: This exercise eliminates the leg action of a regular deadlift, and so isolates the back muscles. It is consequently one of the most thorough exercises for the lower back. First, pick up a barbell in deadlift fashion using your legs and the proper grip. Once you are standing erect, lower the weight by bending at the waist, and touch the barbell to the floor (Illus. 20a). Then, straighten up again, but without using your legs (Illus. 20b). Remember that this is an all-back movement. Start stiff-legged deadlifts with a light weight to determine the condition of your back.

3–5 sets; 5–10 reps

Bent-over rowing: This exercise puts resistance on the lower back while actively working the middle and upper portions. Bend over at the waist to pick up a barbell from the floor and let it hang from your extended

Illus. 21a—Bent-over rowing is a good exercise for all areas of the back as well as the arms.

Illus. 21b—Simply bring the bar up to your chest and then lower it.

arms while you remain bent over (Illus. 21a). Use your arms to pull the bar up as close as possible to your chest (Illus. 21b), then lower it. Even though your arms are doing much of the work, there is still ample use of the middle back in this exercise. For variety, you can use two dumbbells, or one heavy dumbbell while you balance yourself by holding onto a bench with your free hand.

3–5 sets; 5–10 reps

Hyperextensions: This exercise is really the reverse movement of a sit-up. The emphasis is on the lower back region. Lie on a bench, stomach down with your upper body extended over the edge and lock your feet firmly, either by having someone hold them or by using an apparatus designed for this exercise. Lie so that your trunk is free to move, clasp your hands behind your neck and lower your trunk as far as possible (Illus. 22a). Now raise your trunk up as far as you can (Illus. 22b).

When you become stronger at hyperextensions, you can hold weights behind your head for added resistance.

3–5 sets; 10–20 reps

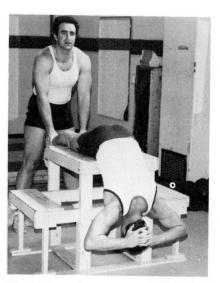 

Illus. 22a and b—Hyperextensions are great for the lower back. From the position shown, lower your upper body and then raise it as far as possible.

Wide-grip pull-ups: By pulling yourself up to a bar while using a wide overhand grip, you can work and strengthen the latissimus dorsi muscles (lats), the middle back just beneath the shoulders. End your pull-ups with your chin over the bar, or, better yet, with the back of your head in front of and over the bar (Illus. 23).

2–3 sets; 5–10 reps

Illus. 23 (left)—Wide-grip pull-ups develop the middle back as well as the arms.
Illus. 24 (right)—The lat machine will also work the middle back.

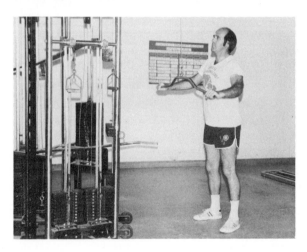

Illus. 25—The lat-machine bar can be pulled down either in front of or behind your head.

Lat-machine pull-downs: Another excellent means of developing strength in the latissimus dorsi muscles is to use a lat-machine, which is a pulley device that is part of the Universal Gym®. Grip the bar with your hands at least as wide apart as your shoulders. Pull the bar down to either the front or the rear of your body (Illus. 24). Pulling the bar behind your head will give a more thorough workout to the lats (Illus. 25). When you have completed the downward movement, allow the weight to return to resting position with resistance so that you work your lats throughout the entire movement.

3–5 sets; 10 reps

Illus. 26a and b—Shoulder shrugs condition the very upper back and the base of the neck.

Shoulder shrugs: Exercise the trapezius muscles at the base of the neck using shrugging movement with a barbell. Hold the barbell at your thighs with an overhand grip so that the weight of the bar is pulling your shoulders down (Illus. 26a). Now, with only the upward movement of your shoulders, raise the bar as far as possible (which will be only a few inches) (Illus. 26b). Lower the barbell to the starting position. You can also do shoulder shrugs with heavy dumbbells.

3–5 sets; 10–20 reps

Developing the Chest

The chest muscles (the pectorals) play a large role in powerlifting. But everyone should be interested in this group of exercises since increased chest size and lung capacity are conducive to appearance and health. In the following exercises, breathing instructions will be specifically detailed. When directly working the regions of the lungs, expansion at the proper time is important.

Bench presses: The best chest developer of them all is the bench press, which is also one of the powerlifts (described in greater detail on pages 99–103). To perform the exercise, lie on your back on a bench, preferably one that has upright racks at one end to hold a barbell. Reach up to remove the bar from the racks, or have a partner hand you a bar, and hold it with extended arms over your head (Illus. 27a). Use a grip anywhere from shoulder-width to about 12 inches wider, and be certain to wrap

34

your thumbs around the bar. Lower the bar, breathing in to expand your chest, touch your chest lightly with the bar (Illus. 27b), and press the bar up fully. Restrict this exercise to your chest muscles by keeping your feet flat on the floor and your buttocks on the bench throughout the entire movement. Besides the pectoral muscles of the chest, the bench press assists in the development of the shoulders and upper arms.

Many gymnasiums have a Universal Gym® on which a bench press can be done. With such a machine you do not have to be concerned about balancing a bar and so it is a good introduction to the bench press.

5 sets; 5–10 reps

Illus. 27a—The bench press is also a competition powerlift. It is the best exercise of all for building up the chest.

Illus. 27b—Lower the bar to your chest while inhaling and raise it while exhaling.

Inclined bench presses: The normal bench press exercises the pectoral region in general. The inclined bench press places the emphasis on the upper pecs. A special incline board or bench is needed for this exercise and usually the help of one or two spotters to hand you the bar. Lower the bar from the extended-arm position, lightly touch the chest, and press upward (Illus. 28). Inhale on the descent and exhale while pressing. The wider the grip, the more the pressing effort is concentrated on your chest rather than the upper arms (triceps). For another variation of the bench press, try doing it on a decline (head lower than your chest). This gives a super workout to the lower pecs.

3–5 sets; 5–10 reps

Illus. 28—The inclined bench press emphasizes the upper pectoral muscles.

Dumbbell bench presses: Lie on a bench and hold a dumbbell in each hand over your chest with straight arms (Illus. 29a). Lower the dumbbells vertically as far as your chest muscles permit, breathing in throughout the movement (Illus. 29b). Then, press the bells straight up in good form, exhaling until completion. You may choose to temporarily substitute this chest-developing exercise for the bench press using a barbell.

3–5 sets; 5–10 reps

Illus. 29a—This variation of the bench press allows the weight to be lowered further.

Illus. 29b—Remember to inhale while lowering the weight and exhale while raising it.

Laterals: This exercise, sometimes referred to as "flyes," will really stretch out and build up the pecs. Lie on a bench and hold a dumbbell in each hand with your arms straight over your chest (Illus. 30a). Now, spread your arms apart as though they were wings, inhaling and lowering the weights through a 90° arc, and farther if your chest muscles allow (Illus. 30b). Then, with the strength of your pectorals, bring the dumbbells together again overhead, exhaling while doing so. Depending on the weight you use, you can do these laterals with either straight arms or with your elbows bent (Illus. 31). Moreover, you can do straight-arm and bent-arm laterals on an incline or decline board.

3–5 sets; 10 reps

37

Illus. 30a—Laterals are excellent for developing the pectorals. Start with the dumbbells over your chest . . .

Illus. 30b— . . . and extend them out to the sides. Then return to the original position.

Illus. 31—A variation of the exercise with the elbows bent. Laterals can also be done inclined or declined.

Pullovers: This is a tough exercise, but worth the trouble. It not only aids chest development, but also works on the upper back and shoulders. Lie on a bench so that your head is near one end, your feet flat on the floor or locked around the legs of the bench. Hold a barbell with straight arms over your chest and with a shoulder-width grip (Illus. 32a). Keep your arms straight, lower the barbell over and in back of your head through at least a 90° arc (Illus. 32b). Inhale throughout. Return the weight by pulling it up and over your head to its starting position over your chest. Exhale while pulling up. Initially, it may be more comfortable to do this when lying on the floor rather than on a bench. Alternatively, you can do the pullover with bent arms (Illus. 33) or use dumbbells instead of a barbell.

3–5 sets; 5–10 reps

Illus. 32a—Pullovers are great for the chest, upper back and shoulders.

Illus. 32b—Bringing the bar back up from this position is tougher than it looks.

Illus. 33—With heavy weights, pullovers can be done with bent elbows.

Shaping Up the Shoulders

Without proper shoulder strength, you will find yourself limited in the competitive arena. Many of the contested lifts center on the pulling and pressing action of the shoulder region. Fortunately, there are a number of ways to shape up your shoulders.

Military presses: Always popular among weightlifters, the military press offers a prime means of developing the shoulders. With feet about shoulder-width apart, grasp a barbell with an overhand grip and bring it to your shoulders (Illus. 34a). (The proper way to do this, or "clean" a barbell, is

Illus. 34a and b—The military press simply requires you to push the bar from your chest to an overhead position. It can be done standing or seated.

discussed on pages 67–71.) Push the bar vertically until your arms are fully extended overhead (Illus. 34b). Lower and repeat. You can do these presses either standing or sitting. Sitting presses are difficult because you can't "cheat" by using your body.

3–5 sets; 5–8 reps

Presses behind the neck: This is a variation of the military press. It concentrates more on the backs of the shoulders than the regular "militaries" do. Place a barbell at the rear of your neck (or have someone else put it there for you), with your palms face up (Illus. 35a). Press the bar up until your arms are fully extended. Keep the barbell behind your head (Illus. 35b). Lower and repeat. Like the military press, you can do this press standing or seated.

3–5 sets; 5–8 reps

Illus. 35a and b—Pressing behind the neck places more emphasis on the back of the shoulders.

Dumbbell presses: Pressing with dumbbells rather than with a bar puts a little more demand on the sides of the shoulders. Dumbbell presses can be done standing, sitting, by pressing one arm at a time, or by pressing left and right arms simultaneously or alternately (Illus. 36).

3–5 sets; 5–10 reps

Upright rowing: This exercise gives a thorough workout to the entire shoulder region. Hold a barbell at your thighs with arms extended (Illus. 37a). Pulling the barbell directly up, parallel to your body, as far as possible (Illus. 37b), and then lower it. Maintain a smooth pull throughout

Illus. 36—For variety in pressing overhead, use dumbbells while standing or
sitting.

the movement and keep the bar close to your body. The pulling in this exercise simulates rowing a boat, hence the name "upright rowing." Besides helping the shoulders, this rowing action greatly assists the trapezius muscles at the base of the neck and tops of the shoulders.

3–5 sets; 7–10 reps

Illus. 37a and b—For upright rowing, pull the bar directly up using the shoulders.

Front lateral raises: Lateral raises place a tremendous demand on the front deltoids. Hold a barbell at your thighs with your arms extended

(Illus. 38a). Then, with only the strength of your shoulders, raise the weight forward until your arms are at least parallel to the floor (Illus. 38b). You can also do front lateral raises with dumbbells. Raise both arms together or alternately. For stricter control, do front lateral raises with dumbbells while seated on the edge of a bench.

3 sets; 7–10 reps

Illus. 38a—The front deltoids really get a workout with this exercise.

Illus. 38b—Raise a barbell or the dumbbells straight out in front of you using shoulder strength alone.

Side lateral raises: To put the emphasis on the side deltoids, raise dumbbells with arms straight directly out from the sides of your body (Illus. 39a and b). Go at least as high as horizontal, then lower the weight to your thighs and repeat. Side lateral raises can be done one arm at a time or two simultaneously.

3 sets; 7–10 reps

Illus. 39a—This exercise will build the side deltoids.

Illus. 39b— Simply raise the dumbbells out to the sides.

Bent-over lateral raises: The best exercise for the posterior deltoids or the rear shoulder muscles is a lateral raise with dumbbells while leaning over. Take a dumbbell in each hand and bend over at the waist, letting the weights hang from your arms (Illus. 40a). Use the muscles at the back of your shoulders to raise the dumbbells up so that your arms are parallel to the ground (Illus. 40b). Lower the weights and repeat.

3 sets; 7–10 reps

Illus. 40b—Try to maintain this position for about one second during each rep.

Activating the Arms

The upper arm muscles, the biceps and triceps, need to be conditioned for competitive weightlifting, too. Although most beginners are more interested in developing the biceps, it is really the triceps that should be emphasized. Triceps play the larger role in pulling and pressing and they form two thirds of the upper arm compared to only one third for the biceps.

Curls: Barbell curls for the biceps have long been the mainstay of arm exercises. Simply hold a barbell with a shoulder-width palms-up grip. Curl the bar up to touch your shoulders (Illus. 41), and back down. To do biceps curls properly, you should keep your back straight and concentrate on using only your upper arms to curl the bar. When lowering the bar, remain firm and slightly resist the pull of the bar.

3–5 sets; 5–10 reps

Illus. 41—Remember to use only biceps action while curling. Keep back and hips steady.

Illus. 42 and 43—Use of dumbbells can add some variety to this exercise. Dumbbell curls can be done seated or on an incline as well as standing.

Dumbbell curls: To get a somewhat different movement for the curling exercise, use dumbbells instead of a barbell. With dumbbells, you can curl standing, seated (Illus. 42), or on an incline (Illus. 43). Exercise each arm alternately, or both arms simultaneously.

3–5 sets; 8–10 reps

Illus. 44a—Using a narrow grip for bench pressing concentrates on the triceps.

Illus. 44b—The movement is the same as for a normal bench press.

Narrow-grip bench presses: Although the bench press is primarily a chest exercise, you can narrow your grip to emphasize your triceps. Except for the close spacing of the hands, this movement is performed exactly like the normal bench press (pages 34–35). The bar is picked off the rack at the head of the bench, lowered to touch your chest (Illus. 44a), and pressed fully upward (Illus. 44b).

2–4 sets; 5–10 reps

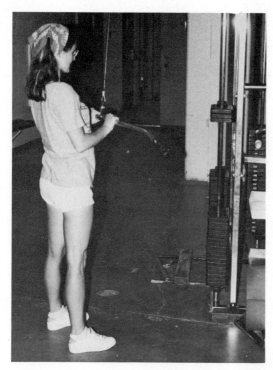

Illus. 45—Keeping the elbows fixed while using the lat machine isolates the triceps.

Lat-machine press-downs: By using a narrow grip on the lat-machine pulley (part of the Universal Gym®), you can isolate your triceps for an intense workout (Illus. 45). Remember to keep your elbows stationary so that shoulder movement is not brought in to assist in the press-down. When your arms are fully extended, lower the weights, but resist them to get full benefit from the exercise.

3–5 sets; 8–10 reps

Illus. 46—When doing standing triceps extensions, be sure not to bring unnecessary muscles into the movement.

Illus. 47a and b—If you remember not to move your elbows, this exercise will nicely isolate the triceps.

Triceps extensions: This exercise also isolates the triceps, provided you can keep your elbows stationary. Sit on the edge of a bench and hold a dumbbell behind your neck (Illus. 47a). Then, *without moving your elbows,* raise the weight above the back of your head and lower (Illus. 47b). You can also do this movement holding a barbell with a narrow grip (Illus. 46). This is sometimes called a "French press." You can also perform it while lying on a bench. In this latter case, hold a bar over your chest and lower it, elbows fixed, to your forehead, and raise again (Illus. 48). The key for any of these extensions is to keep your elbows fixed.

3–5 sets; 5–10 reps

Illus. 48—This exercise can also be done in a variety of ways.

Dips: Raising and lowering your body by holding on between parallel bars is a combination triceps-deltoid-pectoral exercise. Position yourself between the bars, leap up, bringing yourself off the floor and holding the bars with straight arms (Illus. 49a). Using your upper arms and shoulders, lower yourself in a controlled manner as far as possible (Illus. 49b), and then recover to your original position. If the bars are too low for you to dip down fully, simply bend your legs back.

3–5 sets; 10 reps

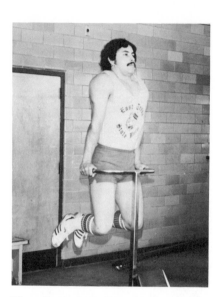 

Illus. 49a and b—Dips are fine for the triceps, chest and shoulders. If your legs are too long to clear the floor, simply bend your knees as shown.

Improving the Stomach Muscles

Almost every competitive lift puts a demand on the stomach region and down through the groin. In addition, improving your stomach muscles will greatly enhance your appearance.

Sit-ups: The most fundamental and perhaps the best stomach exercise is the sit-up. There are many ways to improve the effectiveness of this movement and variations to change its effect. Start first by lying flat on your back (hands behind the head) and place your feet beneath a somewhat immovable object. If you are at home, place your feet beneath a piece of furniture or a barbell. At the gym, the available sit-up board will have a place for your feet. After that, all you do is sit up from that prone position using the pull of your stomach muscles (Illus. 50). Bend your trunk over far enough so that you touch your elbows to your knees. For

added resistance, hold a weight behind your head, do them on an incline
board, or do sit-ups with your knees bent.

1–3 sets; 20–50 reps

Illus. 50—The sit-up is the simplest and best exercise for the abdominal muscles. Doing them on an incline makes them a bit more challenging.

Hanging leg raises: Hang from a chinning bar or from the special handles
of a Universal Gym® (Illus. 51a). Isolate your stomach muscles by raising
your legs until they are at least perpendicular to your trunk (Illus. 51b). For
variety, bring your knees into your stomach.

1–3 sets; 10–15 reps

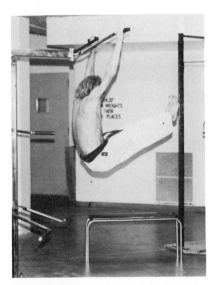

Illus. 51a and b—Hanging leg raises are tougher than they look. Try to get your legs perpendicular to your body.

Leg raises: This is the opposite movement of a sit-up. In this case, you keep your trunk fixed and raise and lower your legs at the waist (Illus. 52a). Bring your legs up until they are perpendicular to your body (Illus. 52b). You can do leg raises from a horizontal position or on an incline. Use an incline board that provides a handhold.

1–3 sets; 10–25 reps

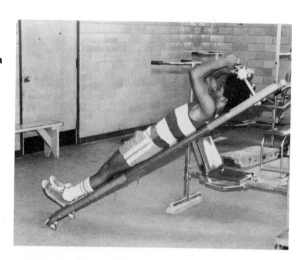

Illus. 52a—Leg raises on an incline are more difficult than on the level, but are worth the effort.

Illus. 52b—Again, get your legs perpendicular to your body to form an "L."

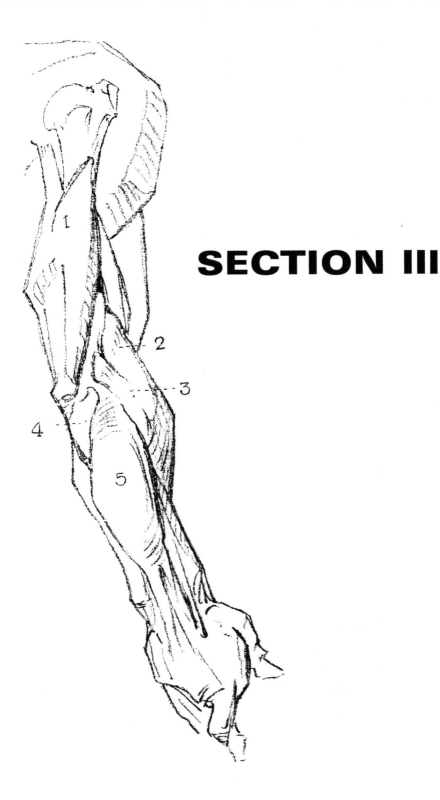

SECTION III

Olympic Lifts

The snatch and the clean and jerk are truly the granddaddies of competitive weightlifting, both having been performed in competition in Paris in 1924. There were other lifts used during competitions at that time, but over the years competition has been narrowed to these two.

Present-day Olympic lifters are able to concentrate their training, and the results have been impressive, showing up especially during the quadrennial Olympics. For example, the world record for the clean and jerk in the super-heavyweight class in 1964 was 479 lb. (216 kg.). In 1976 that record had been pushed up to 562 lb. (255 kg.), a remarkable 17 per cent increase in strength and technique in a period of 12 years. With serious and diligent training at the Olympic lifts, there is no telling what weights can be ultimately snatched and clean-and-jerked.

Needless to say, over-all body strength helps make a superb Olympic lifter, but there is much more to the Olympic lifts than mere strength. From the moment the bar is pulled off the floor, that strength must be steadily shifted, flowing up from the legs through the back and chest muscles to the shoulders and finally up through the outstretched arms to the wrists. The two competitive lifts, the two-hands snatch and the two-hands clean and jerk, call on nearly every muscle group of the body to contribute to the lift, but this strength will be squandered if the lifter cannot also provide a healthy share of co-ordination, flexibility, balance, and speed.

Never sacrifice form and style for strength when learning and practicing Olympic lifts. Use a light weight when you begin, so that you can perfect the proper technique. Careful study and practice of the Olympic lifts presented here will get you onto the lifting platform in fine style far sooner than you may think possible, and enable you to progress steadily to conquer heavier and heavier weights.

Safety notes: The impatient, hasty, and careless individual will surely be injured performing Olympic lifts just as he would while rashly participating in any other sport. Olympic lifting is not dangerous, but a careless lifter might claim that it is. Safety requires that you respect the weight on the bar and understand your personal strength at any given time.

When learning the fundamentals of these lifts, work only with weights you can handle quite easily, and only after you are sufficiently stretched and warmed up. Later, when you have progressed and are reasonably adept at the sport, you should have no problem when you attempt to lift heavier poundages. At any point in an Olympic lift, the bar can be safely dropped without coming in contact with your body. Be careful not to lift a bar before others are well clear.

The Grip

You must be able to hold the bar securely if you are to pull weights successfully. Many lifters find that an ordinary overhand grip, with the thumb encircling the bar, is just not adequate. Therefore, the grip commonly used for Olympic lifts is a "hook" grip, with the thumb placed around the bar and underneath the index and second fingers (Illus. 53). At first, you may find the hook grip unusual and uncomfortable, but with practice, it will become more and more natural. More important, it will pay off later in your lifting career when you need added strength in your grip for lifting your maximum poundages. Also, use plenty of chalk on your hands for added security.

The Snatch

Of all the weightlifting movements, the snatch is considered the most difficult because it requires you to lift the weight overhead in one continuous motion. Fast reflexes and good shoulder and ankle mobility are intrinsic attributes needed for the snatch, but tremendous contributions are also expected from the legs and back. Any lifter who can snatch about one-and-a-half times his bodyweight is doing very well.

There are two methods used to perform the snatch, which differ in the placement of the feet when hoisting the bar overhead. The most popular style is called the *squat-style snatch*. A less frequently used technique is referred to as the *split-style snatch*. Because of the uncommon usage of the split-style snatch, the instructional emphasis here is placed on the squat-style snatch.

The squat-style snatch will generally allow you to lift heavier poundages, but balance becomes more of a problem. Therefore, many squat-style lifters use shoes with heels to help them keep their balance during this lift.

Illus. 53—The hook grip will give you a firmer hold on the bar, necessary for lifting heavy weights.

Object of the Snatch

In the snatch, the barbell must be lifted from a horizontal position in front of the lifter's legs to a position over his head with his arms vertically outstretched *in one continuous motion*. Although halfway through the movement, the lifter acquires a stooped or squatted position (for the squat-style snatch), or a split-legged position (for the split-style snatch), the final position is that of an erect stance. During competition, the bar must be held overhead under control for about two seconds, until the referee commands "down."

Performance of the Squat-Style Snatch

The barbell is placed horizontally on a wooden platform or a thick rubber mat. Approach the barbell and place your feet so that your shins are slightly behind the bar. Your heels should be about shoulder-width apart and your toes pointed out slightly. However, you may wish to vary your stance, depending on your personal preference.

The set position before the bar is critical for a good pull and requires perfect positioning of several body parts. Reach down to grasp the bar with an overhand (palms down) grip substantially wider than shoulder-width (Illus. 54a). A wide grip allows for maximum flexibility in the shoulders, although if the grip is excessively wide, the pull on the bar becomes less efficient. Remember to use a hook grip.

When set, your shins should lightly brush the bar, your arms should be nearly perpendicular to the floor and straight, and your shoulders slightly in front of the bar. The position of your shoulders is important. Be sure to lean far enough forward to get your shoulders in front of the bar.

Drop your hips so that your buttocks are as low as comfortably possible. Your entire back should be flat or slightly arched and not hunched (Illus. 54b). Position your head so that you are looking directly ahead, and note that your body is still over the bar so that your shoulders are slightly in front of your hands. Keep your arms straight.

With most of the weight of your body on the balls of your feet, begin the pull on the bar by driving with your legs (hips, buttocks, and thigh

Illus. 54a and b—To begin the snatch, make sure your grip is wide, your back flat, and your shoulders slightly in front of the bar.

muscles), while keeping your back flat (Illus. 55a). Do not raise your buttocks before the bar leaves the platform or you will lose some of the driving power of the legs. Keep your head up. Your arms should remain taut but somewhat relaxed.

The initial pull should not be explosive, but rather moderately fast and controlled. If you pull too quickly, the bar will tend to be forced too far to the front of your body.

Illus. 55a and b—During the initial pull, maintain the straight back and the forward position of the shoulders. The pull should be controlled rather than explosive.

As the barbell approaches your knees, your buttocks will begin to rise, but keep your back flat to maximize the strength of your legs and hips (Illus. 55b). Your shoulders should still be slightly in front of the bar.

As the bar passes your knees, your body must be kept in close to the bar, and the bar may actually brush against your thighs. The bar must rise in as straight a vertical line as possible. This is made possible by moving your hips forward as your body rises (Illus. 56a and 56b).

When the bar is near the level of your waist, your hips should be moved completely in towards the bar, thus straightening out your body. You should also assist the pull by starting to rise on the balls of your feet. This is commonly referred to as the "second pull."

As the bar passes the hip region and you are on the balls of your feet, your body should be nearly vertical (Illus. 57b). Remember to keep your body close to the bar. At this point, your body is at its full extended position, your back and legs are straight, and your elbows will begin to break (Illus. 57a). Do not lean back to assist the pull, but remain as close

Illus. 56a and b—As the bar approaches your waist, bring your hips close to the bar, which should be rising in a vertical plane.

to the vertical as possible. (Some lighter weightlifters sometimes have to compensate for a heavy weight by leaning back slightly at the end of their pull.) Do *not* break your elbows before reaching an extended position on the balls of your feet.

When the weight reaches chest level, your arms are strongly bent at the elbows and your shoulders are shrugged upward, both allowing for the

Illus. 57a and b—Rise upwards on the balls of your feet as you approach the top of the pull. Your body should be straight and your elbows beginning to break.

Illus. 58a and b—At the top of the pull, begin to drop beneath the bar as your wrists start to whip the bar over.

maximum pull on the bar (Illus. 58a). At the moment of the maximum pull, begin to descend beneath the bar to a squat position and whip the bar over with your wrists (Illus. 59a and b). This movement somewhat resembles pulling yourself under the bar as though swinging on a "jungle gym." The descent must be a continuous movement without hesitation. Do not turn your wrists until your head has passed beneath the bar. Pull the bar high enough before you begin to drop below it.

Illus. 59a and b—The descent should give you the feeling of "swinging" on the bar as your body moves downward and the bar moves up and back.

Illus. 60a and b—The descent finishes in a stable full-squat position with arms locked and the bar over the back of your head.

The descent beneath the bar leads to a squat, or "sitting down," position with a full knee bend (Illus. 60a). The impact of the weight overhead is cushioned mainly by your hips before you reach bottom.

Actually, a lifter must acquire a feel for when the absolute limit on the pull has been reached and to descend beneath the bar at that split second. While dropping beneath the bar, ram your arms up to lock the bar overhead. Remember to keep looking straight ahead.

Illus. 61a and b—Use your legs to drive up out of the squat and achieve an erect stance—the final position of the snatch.

Pause momentarily in the squat position to catch perfect balance of your body and the barbell overhead (although many times a pause is not necessary, depending on how near perfect your descent is). Ideally, the bar should be directly over the back of your head (Illus. 60b). If the bar is a little off, adjust your position by slightly moving your head and shoulders. If the bar is forward, raise your head a small amount. If the bar is too far back, lower your head and drop your shoulders slightly forward. In any case, keep your back flat and nearly erect and your arms stretched straight up.

To complete the squat lift, you must drive out of the squat position to an erect stance, keeping your arms locked and overhead with the bar (Illus. 61a). When a snatch is performed properly, the lifter can sometimes "bounce" right out of the squat without losing his balance.

Key Points of the Squat-Style Snatch

● When getting into set position, lean over the bar and keep your back flat and hips low. Look straight ahead.

● Pull the bar up in a vertical plane.

● Don't pull the bar into your body but stay close to the bar. Bring your hips "into" the bar as it passes your knees and as you straighten.

● Keep driving with your legs, hips, and back until you are up on your toes.

● Do not break your arms at the elbows until you are up on the balls of your feet and at the peak of your body extension.

● While extended, keep your body nearly vertical. Do not lean backwards.

● Do not turn your wrists before your head goes below the bar.

● Keep looking straight ahead throughout the movement.

Performance of the Split-Style Snatch

The fundamentals of the pull for the split-style snatch are identical to those for the squat-style snatch (Illus. 54 to Illus. 57) except that your feet can be closer together and the pull must be slightly higher. The major difference between the two styles of snatching is the descent of the lifter's body beneath the bar.

At the moment of the maximum pull (when the bar is about chest-high) the legs are quickly split, one forward and the other backward, and the body begins to move beneath the bar. The legs should *not* be split so that they fall in a direct line, one behind the other. One foot must lie sufficiently to the right of the other to enable you to keep your balance.

Your feet should end well apart, the front leg bent at the knee with the knee forward over the toes. Your rear leg should stretch back with a slight bend at the knee. Do *not* bend your knee to touch the platform. That would disqualify you in a contest. Only the ball of that rear foot will be touching the platform. Your trunk should remain erect with the arms holding the bar overhead. Ideally, an imaginary straight line would pass from the bar through the rear of your head to your shoulders. To help obtain and retain this proper form and balance, your head must face directly ahead.

The final stage of the split-style snatch is the recovery from the split. This requires you to straighten both legs before you move your feet. When your knees are no longer bent, you will have a solid footing and will be able to bring your feet together in small alternating steps, beginning with the front foot, to reach the final erect position with the barbell overhead.

Illus. 62a and b—The split-style snatch is performed in the same manner as the squat-style snatch until you reach the top of the pull. At that point, split your legs apart front to back.

Illus. 62c—Your feet should not end up directly in line with each other. This will make it impossible for you to maintain your balance.

Illus. 62d—At the end of the split, with arms locked overhead, achieve an erect stance by bringing your feet together in small, alternating steps.

Key Points of the Split-Style Snatch

● See "Key Points" for squat-style snatching.

● Move into the split position with speed. Do not hesitate.

● The legs should be split well apart, the front sharply bent at the knee, and the rear extended with a slight bend at the knee. Do not dip so low that you touch the rear knee to the floor.

● To assure balance, do not split your legs one directly behind the other.

● To recover from the split, straighten your knees first.

Special Notes for Competition

(a) Once you begin to lift the bar, do not stop. If the bar passes your knees, that initial movement will be counted as one of your three attempts.

(b) Do not pause at any time during the snatching movement, except in the squat position if this is necessary to catch your balance.

(c) Maintain an even extension of your arms throughout.

(d) Do not turn your wrists to thrust the bar overhead until your head is below the bar.

(e) Do *not* hesitate and then push or press the bar overhead. Finishing with a "press-out" means disqualification. It is essential to lock your arms overhead and keep them locked.

(f) Touching the platform with any part of your body other than your feet will negate the lift.

(g) Remember to wait for the referee's signal before lowering the bar. The signal will not be given, however, until you are perfectly motionless.

(h) Dropping the bar after the signal will negate an otherwise good lift. When lowering the bar, keep your hands on it until it touches the floor. Besides complying with regulations, maintaining at least partial control of the bar helps preserve the equipment.

The Clean and Jerk

The two-hands clean and jerk is, as the name implies, composed of two distinct movements. It is the lift during which an individual can thrust the most weight possible overhead—usually far more than can be accomplished in the snatch. Well-trained lifters in the lighter bodyweight classes can clean and jerk more than twice their bodyweight. The clean and jerk is a lift in which the strength and technique needed for the pull, or clean, are combined with the strength, timing, and co-ordination demanded in the jerk. The result is a highly artistic athletic movement.

Object of the Clean and Jerk

The clean and jerk requires, first, that a barbell be lifted in one continuous motion from a horizontal position in front of the lifter's legs to a temporary position at the shoulders while the lifter achieves an erect stance (the clean). Second, the bar must be thrust in one continuous motion from the shoulders to a final position overhead with outstretched arms (the jerk). During competition, the bar must be held overhead under control for about two seconds, until the referee commands "down."

Performance of the Clean and Jerk

The barbell is placed horizontally on a wooden platform or a thick rubber mat. Approach the bar and place your feet so that your shins are about 2 inches (5 cm.) from the bar. Your heels should be about shoulder-width or somewhat closer and your toes should point slightly outward (Illus. 63a). You may vary the width of your stance later if this is not comfortable.

Get set for the clean by reaching down to grasp the bar with an overhand (palms down) grip outside your legs at about shoulder-width. You may want to try the "hook" grip (page 56) for extra security while holding the bar. Your arms should be extended, straight and almost relaxed, and your shoulders should lean slightly out in front of the bar (Illus. 63b). Keep your buttocks as low as is comfortably possible. Drop your hips and set your back in a flat position. Your head should be up and looking directly ahead, not down at the bar. Check the position of your shoulders. Be sure that you are still leaning over the bar and note that your shins are now lightly brushing the bar.

With your weight on the balls of your feet, begin the pull on the bar by driving with every muscle in your legs—the thighs, buttocks, and hips. Remember in the initial pull to keep your back flat and not to raise your buttocks before the bar leaves the platform. Keep your arms straight and your eyes directly ahead.

Do not rush the initial pull. It should be moderately fast but controlled. If the initial pull on the bar is too explosive, you are likely to pull the bar

Illus. 63a and b—Prepare for the clean and jerk with your back flat and shoulders slightly ahead of the bar.

Illus. 64a and b—The pull should be strong but controlled—not explosive. Keep your back flat and look straight ahead.

too far in front and away from your body. The bar must rise vertically and close to your body.

When the bar is at knee level, your buttocks will begin to rise (Illus. 64a). Keep your back flat so that you can still drive from your legs and hips. Your shoulders should be in front of the bar, as they were when you originally got set at the bar.

Illus. 65a and b—As the bar approaches your waist, your hips will move forward but the bar must continue to rise in a vertical plane.

Illus. 66a and b—At the top of the pull, a strong shoulder shrug is required as you rise onto the balls of your feet.

Once the bar is past your knees, accelerate the pull. The bar must rise in a vertical path from the platform. Keep your body close to the bar. As the bar passes your knees, your hips will begin to move in as your body rises (Illus. 65a and b).

When the bar is just below waist level, your hips should move in completely toward the bar to assist in an accelerated upward thrust of the bar

Illus. 67a and b—As you bend your knees to descend beneath the bar, begin to bring it back to your shoulders.

(Illus. 66a). Start to rise on the balls of your feet as a final extension of the pulling movement.

When the bar passes the hip region, you should be up on the balls of your feet, fully extended upright with shrugged shoulders, and nearly vertical in stance (Illus. 66b). Your arms should break at the elbows and begin to contribute to the pull. It is essential to keep your body close to the bar. Do not lean backwards in an attempt to assist the pull.

Immediately after you have reached full extension, quickly move to drop below the bar by bending at the knees (Illus. 67a). The pull for the clean does not have to be as high as in the snatch, but you must still pull high enough so that your body can drop beneath the bar.

As you descend, whip your wrists around so that your palms face up and the bar is brought into the shoulders (Illus. 68a). While bringing the bar to your shoulders, purposefully point your elbows high and forward. Ideally, your upper arms will be parallel to the floor.

At the end of the clean, the bar should come to a rest position high up on the chest and deltoids and at the base of your throat (at the clavicle) while you descend into a squatting or "sitting down" position. Be sure that while in the squat, your elbows are high enough to avoid touching your thighs and that your back is erect. It is illegal to touch your thighs with your elbows during a contest.

As soon as the weight is balanced, rise out of the squat with power from your legs and hips. End at an erect stance (Illus. 69a). Continue to rest the bar on your upper chest, concentrating on keeping your elbows up. Do not

Illus. 68a and b—At the bottom of the descent, your elbows should be high and pointing forward with the bar at your collarbone.

Illus. 69a and b—The clean portion of the lift is finished by rising out of the squat into an erect stance.

shift your feet while rising, and be sure that they end up on an even line. Stand as erect and tall as possible. This completes the cleaning movement.

The jerk should be made as soon as possible after the clean is completed, but not before you are mentally prepared and are properly balanced. The power for the jerk lies in both the legs and the shoulders. To begin the movement, lower your body about 6 inches (15 cm.) in a controlled dip

Illus. 70a and b—As soon as you have recovered from the clean, begin the jerk with a slight dip of your knees.

by bending your knees (Illus. 70a). It is imperative that the position of the barbell on your shoulders remains undisturbed. As you lower your body, the bar should dip in a vertical plane.

When you reach the bottom of your small dip, spring upward, straightening your legs and thrusting the barbell upward and off your shoulders (Illus. 71a). You may wish to cock your head back slightly to be certain you do not graze your chin with the bar.

Rise on your toes during the springing movement to assist the thrust. At the moment you reach the highest point of your spring, rapidly split your legs, one forward and one backwards (Illus. 72a). The split will lower your body, leaving the barbell above the top of your head.

Illus. 71a and b—Then spring upwards, driving with your legs and thrusting the barbell up off your shoulders.

From the time of the split (and just before your feet are planted firmly on the platform) you need to use all the power in your arms and shoulders to push the weight up and lock your arms overhead. You want the bar to end above your head, slightly behind your ears (Illus. 72b). Do not follow the bar with your eyes, but keep them directly ahead. This will help bring the bar far enough back and over your head to position it for proper balance.

An imaginary line should be able to pass from the bar through the head to the shoulders. If the bar is too far forward or backwards, you will have to "chase" it, and possibly never get the right balance to complete the lift. To help maintain your balance while in the split position, point the toes of your forward foot slightly inward (Illus. 72a).

Illus. 72a and b—Descend under the bar by splitting your legs front to back. At the end of the split, the bar should be locked over the back of your head.

The final step of the jerk is to recover from the split position to one where your feet are together on an even line. Straighten out your legs before moving your feet. Then take small alternating steps with each leg, beginning with the front leg until your feet are together. Hold this erect position with the barbell extended overhead (Illus. 73a).

Illus. 73a and b—Straighten your legs before bringing your feet together. The final position for the clean and jerk is an erect stance.

```
┌──────────────── Key Points of the Clean and Jerk ────────────────┐
```
● When getting into position, lean over the bar and keep your back flat and hips low. Look straight ahead.

● In the pull for the clean, the bar should rise in a vertical plane.

● During the pull, stay close to the bar, bringing your hips into the bar as it passes the knees and, continue to drive with your legs until you are high on the balls of your feet.

● Break your arms at the elbows only when you are at the top of the pull, and not before.

● When extended, your body should be nearly vertical and not leaning backwards. Keep your head up throughout the movement looking straight ahead.

● When you bring the bar back into your shoulders, be certain that your elbows are high and pointed forward.

● Make your dip and spring for the jerk quick and snappy. Do not follow the barbell with your eyes—look straight ahead.

● Try to place the jerked barbell over your head slightly behind the ears. Lock your arms quickly.

Special Notes for Competition

(a) Do not pause at any time during either movement. The clean and the jerk must each be accomplished in one continuous motion.

(b) Do not touch the platform with any part of your body other than your feet. Doing so will disqualify the attempt.

(c) You cannot touch the bar to any part of your body before the clean is completed or touch your knees with your elbows while in the squat position of the clean. Both are infractions of the rules and will negate the lift. The bar can graze the thighs but it cannot have an obvious stop at that point. Also, you cannot use oils or grease to facilitate pulling the bar past your thighs.

(d) You can reposition your grip without penalty once you have cleaned the barbell and are preparing to jerk.

(e) The jerk must be one continuous upward movement with the elbows locked at completion. Keep the extension of your arms even and do not complete the jerk with a "press-out." Once you begin the clean, follow it through. Stopping after the bar passes your knees negates your attempt.

(f) Stepping off the platform with the barbell while trying to obtain your balance will count as an unsuccessful lift.

(g) Do not lower the barbell before the referee's signal. You must be motionless and with your feet in line before you will receive a signal.

(h) Maintain hold of the bar when lowering it. Dropping it outright will ruin an otherwise good lift according to regulations.

Training for Olympic Lifting

Even though there are only two competitive Olympic lifts to train for, there is still controversy and uneasiness among lifters and coaches over what may be the best and most effective training system. Well-established competitors often experiment with training routines if a new training system looks promising. This is not intended to make Olympic lifting sound full of uncertainties, but rather to emphasize that any specific system that works for one lifter may not be an approach that guarantees success for another lifter, over either the long or short term. Depending on an individual's physical and chemical make-up, training systems rarely produce the same results for two different people. Muscular and skeletal arrangements vary from one lifter to another, as do the intensity and determination with which a lifter undertakes his training.

There is not a single, all-encompassing training course suitable for everyone—at least not at the advanced stages. However, there are solid and sensible approaches to Olympic lifting that can be used by all beginners to build a good foundation. With time and progress you will learn to modify a fundamental regimen to suit your individual tastes and needs.

At all times, keep a detailed record of your progress so that you can determine exactly how each lift is improving and which supplementary exercises are working best for you. To reach your full capability as a lifter, you must note any weak points in your training and iron them out.

For the beginner, a three-day-a-week schedule is adequate. Established lifters often put in a fourth day, but these men have been at the sport so long that they have developed their regimes to a fine art and they can tell when they are bordering on over-training. (Over-training is, in fact, the plague of Olympic lifters.) For beginners, a three-day scheme of about one hour each session is substantial. Try a Monday-Wednesday-Friday schedule with the weekends off for full rest.

As a beginner, your regimen should emphasize the Olympic lifts themselves, until each movement becomes as natural to you as running or throwing. As you reach a more advanced level, the supplementary exercises discussed on pages 82–90 should become a substantial part of your training, so that you begin improving your lifts by using exercises that closely resemble the actual lifts.

Before your training can get off the ground, you must determine your maximum poundages for each Olympic lift. The suggested basic training routine on pages 80–81 is based on the percentages of your "bests" at each lift. You cannot, after all, work to your full capacity during every workout. At times, you may be selecting poundages that are only 60 per cent of what you are capable of lifting. Of course, as your strength increases, you must also keep track of the increases in the maximum poundages you can lift for each movement, so that you can recalculate your percentages on that new basis.

Begin your workouts with a variety of warm-ups and emphasize stretching exercises. The importance of stretching for Olympic lifting cannot be overemphasized. Many lifters spend a solid 15 minutes just loosening every muscle and joint in their bodies before starting on the Olympic lifts. Use the sequence of stretching movements that was outlined on pages 22–23 as a basis for this part of your warm-up, and add some of the movements illustrated in Illus. 74–81. Getting as limber as the lifter illustrated, however, will take a little time.

After stretching on a mat, begin to loosen up for the lifts themselves by stretching with a bar. For the snatch, do some very light lifts as preliminary movements. You must be quite loose for the snatch if you want to prevent injury or muscle strain.

The training regimen on pages 80 and 81 specifies the number of sets and reps you should do at a lower weight (indicated by "prep" for preparation), before you reach your maximum for that day (indicated by the percentage listed). The preliminary sets should be done with the weight increasing with each set. The plus (+) signs included in the 100% means that you should try to establish a new maximum at that time. Periodically attempting maximum poundages is important for your ego. Note that as the percentages go up from one workout to another, the number of reps decreases. When you are doing close to your capability, you cannot expect to do more than one rep at a time with sufficient-rest between sets.

Do not think that you must do all of the supplementary exercises listed in each workout. Two per workout should be adequate. Select those exercises, as well as any others from pages 25–52, which will help improve your weak points. The sets and reps listed with the supplementary exercises include all to be done for one work-out, and the percentages refer to percentages of the maximum weights you can handle in each exercise.

By following the proposed schedule, any beginning lifter can quickly move past the novice stage to a point where he or she can begin devising a regimen that better fits his or her personal needs. The scheme here is designed so that you peak at each Olympic lift every third week. To facilitate thorough recovery, only one lift is emphasized in any particular workout. The third day of each week is reserved as a relative day of rest, each lift being only 70 per cent of your maximum.

Whenever you go for your maximum attempt during a particular workout, you should show a gain of 5 to 10 pounds (2.5 to 5 kg.) over your previous best. Recalculate your percentages for the following cycle based on your new maximum weight for either lift.

How long you can make gains on this regimen cannot be predicted. Possibly you can go as long as a year on it. So much depends on variables such as your intrinsic strength. In any case, with steady training and a good written record of your progress, you should be well on your way to your optimum training regimen—and a place on the competition platform.

Illus. 74-81—Stretching movements are essential for weightlifters. Be certain that all muscles and joints are loose before lifting heavy poundages.

Illus. 74

Illus. 75

Stretching Exercises

Illus. 76

Illus. 77

Illus. 78

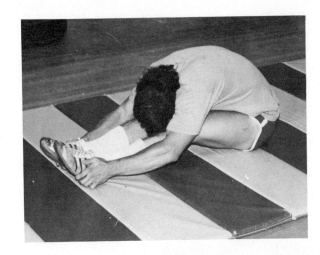

Illus. 79

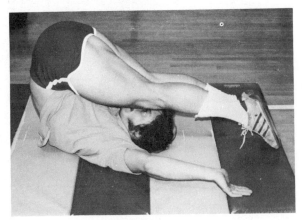

Illus. 80

Illus. 81

Olympic Training Regimen

MONDAY

Week I

Snatch
prep.* 65–75% : 2–3 sets; 3–4 reps
5 ; 4–5

Clean and jerk
prep. 60–70% : 2–3 sets; 3–4 reps
3 ; 4–5

Week II

Snatch
prep. 80–90% : 2–3 sets; 3–4 reps
5 ; 3–4

Clean and jerk
prep. 60–70% : 2–3 sets; 3–4 reps
3 ; 4–5

Week III

Snatch
prep. 95–100+% : 3–4 sets; 2–3 reps
5 ; 1–2

Clean and jerk
prep. 60–70% : 2–3 sets; 3–4 reps
3 ; 4–5

WEDNESDAY

Week I

Snatch
prep. 60–70% : 2–3 sets; 3–4 reps
3 ; 4–5

Clean and jerk
prep. 65–75% : 2–3 sets; 3–4 reps
5 ; 4–5

Week II

Snatch
prep. 60–70% : 2–3 sets; 3–4 reps
3 ; 4–5

Clean and jerk
prep. 80–90% : 2–3 sets; 3–4 reps
5 ; 3–4

Week III

Snatch
prep. 60–70% : 2–3 sets; 3–4 reps
3 ; 4–5

Clean and jerk
prep. 95–100+% : 3–4 sets; 2–3 reps
5 ; 1–2

FRIDAY

Week I

Snatch
prep. 70% : 2–3 sets; 3–4 reps
3–5 ; 4–5

Clean and jerk
prep. 70% : 2–3 sets; 3–4 reps
3–5 ; 4–5

Week II

Snatch
prep. 70% : 2–3 sets; 3–4 reps
3–5 ; 4–5

Clean and jerk
prep. 70% : 2–3 sets; 3–4 reps
3–5 ; 4–5

Week III

Snatch
prep. 70% : 2–3 sets; 3–4 reps
3–5 ; 4–5

Clean and jerk
prep. 70% : 2–3 sets; 3–4 reps
3–5 ; 4–5

* Preparation sets for the weight to be used that day (which is indicated by the percentage of your "best").

Supplementary Exercises†

MONDAY		WEDNESDAY		FRIDAY	
Shrugs	(5 sets; 10–15 reps) (80–90%)	Deadlifts	(5–8 sets; 3–5 reps) (75–90%)	Power snatches	(3–5 sets; 3–5 reps) (50–75%)
Power cleans	(3–5 sets; 3–5 reps) (50–90%)	Jerk from rack	(5 sets; 3–5 reps) (80–100+%)	Front squats	(5–8 sets; 5 reps) (60–90%)
Squats	(5–8 sets; 5 reps) (60–90%)	Hyperextensions	(3–5 sets; 10–20 reps)	Sit-ups	(1–2 sets; 20–30 reps, depending on weighted or not)
Presses	(4–5 sets; 5 reps) (75–90%)	Hang snatches	(3–5 sets; 3–5 reps) (50–80%)	Snatch pulls	(5–6 sets; 3–5 reps) (50–100+%)
		Cleans	(3–5 sets; 3–5 reps) (50–100+%)	Overhead squats	(5–8 sets; 5 reps) (60–90%)

† Choose two exercises for each workout.

Supplementary Exercises for the Olympic Lifts

Besides perfecting your lifting techniques and increasing your strength by doing the Olympic lifts themselves, you must also use certain proven exercises that will help you reach your optimum performance.

Below, you will find the key supplementary exercises that champion Olympic lifters used in their routines to build up strength in the body areas so vital to top performance. Several sets of about 5 reps of these movements with a heavy barbell will help improve anyone's Olympic lifting.

Once you become familiar with these supplementary exercises, you can begin to concentrate on those that seem most effective and replace any that seem to have lost their effectiveness or were initially ineffective. Also supplement your training with the general exercises described on pages 25–52, and add any that seem to be beneficial. Keep them in your schedule for at least two months.

Exercises for Both Olympic Lifts

Both the snatch and the clean and jerk require leg and back strength. The following exercises emphasize development of those body areas.

Squat: The snatch and the clean and jerk both require the lifter first to pull the bar to the region of the chest and then to descend beneath it into a squatting position. Full squats will develop the strength needed to maintain that "sitting" position and particularly to recover from it into an erect stance. They help add the necessary power to your thighs, buttocks, and lower back.

The fundamentals of the squat are described in detail on pages 95–99. With heavy weights, squats can only be done with the aid of a rack or squat stands on which the bar can be placed at shoulder height. Also make sure you have a spotter if you are trying a heavy weight.

Front squats: Also a deep knee bend performed with a barbell, the front squat more closely simulates the actual Olympic lifts, since the barbell is held at the clavicle in the exact position of the clean (Illus. 82). As for regular squats, you will need a rack or squat stands on which you rest the bar before and after the movement. While performing this exercise, remember to keep your elbows high as you would after an actual clean. Front squats are an excellent movement for developing the quadriceps (the tops of the thighs) which are the source of much of the driving power used to recover from the bottom positions of snatches and cleans.

Illus. 82—Front squats will help your recovery portions of the Olympic lifts.

Hyperextensions: Great strength and endurance in the lower back can be developed by including hyperextensions in your routine. See page 32 for the details of this movement.

First perform hyperextensions with your hands clasped behind your neck. As you become more proficient, hold weight-plates behind your neck to offer more resistance.

Deadlifts: The deadlift is described in detail on pages 103–106. Instrumental in developing leg and back strength, it will help you develop the strength needed for the initial pull. While deadlifts are usually performed using one overhand and one underhand grip on the bar, you may choose to use an overhand grip with both hands to better simulate the action in the Olympic lifts. Lifters are able to deadlift far more weight than they could ever pull or clean, which is one reason why this is such a good supplementary exercise for the snatch and the clean and jerk.

Shoulder shrugs: The action of the trapezius muscles of the upper back plays an extremely important role at the height of the pulling movement during the pulls for both Olympic lifts. Develop strength for the peaks of your pulls by isolating those muscles, concentrating on shrugging exercises using a moderately heavy barbell. See page 34 for details on shoulder shrugs.

Sit-ups: There is a great strain on the lower stomach and groin area after reaching the bottom position in both the snatch and the clean and jerk. Include sit-ups in your Olympic training routine to develop strength in the lower trunk area. When starting, do regular sit-ups on a horizontal surface. As you progress, do them on an incline board, and, with further

progress, use the incline board and hold a weight-plate behind your neck for maximum resistance (Illus. 83).

Special Exercises for the Snatch

The greatest exercises for the snatch are pulling movements that closely resemble the movements of the lift itself.

Power snatches: This exercise differs from the actual snatch lift only by the omission of the full bottom position. The grip (Illus. 84a) and the initial pull (Illus. 84b) are the same. However, you pull the bar directly into an overhead position while assuming an erect stance (Illus. 84c). To cushion your body from the effect of the weight, make a slight dip with your knees as you lock the bar overhead. Use a weight no greater than about 75 per cent of your best snatch to date.

Snatch pulls: The ability to pull heavy weights fast and high is the mark of a solid Olympic lifter. You can greatly increase your shoulder and upper back strength by working on only the first half of the snatch, the pull. Pull the weight from the floor up to a point where you rise on your toes and break your elbows (Illus. 85). Lower the weight to the floor and repeat.

Overhead squats: Use this exercise to improve your recovery from the squat position of the snatch. Hold the bar overhead as you would after completing a snatch (Illus. 86a) and do deep knee bends, dipping as low as possible to simulate the bottom position of the snatching movement (Illus. 86b).

Hang snatches: Concentrate on the latter half of the snatching move-ment in order to perfect the descent beneath the bar and the fixing of the

Illus. 84a—Use less weight for a power snatch than for a regular snatch.

Illus. 84b—The preparation and pull are the same as before.

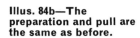

Illus. 84c—Bend your knees to cushion the weight, but a full squat is not necessary.

Illus. 85 (left)—Practice snatch pulls to develop pulling strength.

Illus. 86a and b (below)—Overhead squats simulate the recovery movement of the squat-style snatch.

bar overhead. Omit the pull from the floor, and begin with the bar at your knees (Illus. 87a). Use a weight lighter than your best snatch. Include the bottom position (Illus. 87b) at your discretion.

Illus. 87a—For the hang snatch, start with the bar at hip level. The bar may rest on supports if you like.

Illus. 87b—The movement simulates the latter part of the snatch and the descent beneath the bar.

Special Exercises for the Clean and Jerk

The following are supplementary exercises used to assist in the two discrete parts of this lift.

Power cleans: Clean the barbell without going down into the full bottom position. Bring the bar up from the floor and move directly into an erect stance, using a slight dip at the knees to aid in catching the bar at the chest (Illus. 88). Do power cleans with a weight lighter than you use for your normal cleans.

Clean pulls: Develop better pulling power and learn to bring heavier weights off the floor by working only on the pulling movement of the clean. Bring the bar up from the floor until you are extended on the balls of your feet and have broken your arms at the elbows. This is a great

Illus. 88—Do power cleans with a weight lighter than normal.

Illus. 89a—The jerk from the rack can be done with heavier than normal poundages.

Illus. 89b—This will rapidly improve your maximum clean and jerk weight.

exercise for increasing strength in the middle and upper back, the source for much of the strength needed for heavy cleans.

Jerk from the rack: Work on your jerking power by isolating that part of the clean and jerk lift. With the aid of a rack or squat stands, remove the bar and immediately assume a "cleaned" position (Illus. 89a). Proceed with the jerk as you normally would (Illus. 89b). Because you have expended no energy in cleaning the bar, you should be able to jerk much

Illus. 90—Olympic lifting requires more than strength. It demands speed, agility, and co-ordination as well.

greater poundages than normal. In fact, you should concentrate on making rapid improvements over your previous bests.

Military presses: Increased shoulder and arm strength for the jerk can be accomplished by working military presses (see pages 40–41). Although a much slower movement than the jerk, this exercise will help establish greater strength in the regions of the body that are used when jerking, namely, the triceps, the deltoids and the trapezius muscles. For variation and for greater discipline in form, try pressing from a seated position.

Presses behind the neck: This is a variation of the military press (see page 40). Hold the weight at the back of the neck rather than the upper chest and emphasize the rear deltoids and trapezius muscles. The press behind the neck can be done standing or sitting and it can be done as alternate reps with the military presses within one set of presses.

Illus. 91—Practice and perseverance will give you a measure of satisfaction in weightlifting—and maybe a shelfful of trophies besides.

SECTION IV

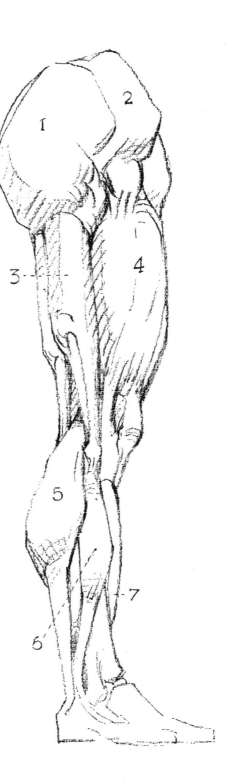

The Powerlifts

The three powerlifts test and develop the body's major muscle groups—the legs, the chest, and the back. It is the strength of these prime areas that mainly determines how much weight you will ultimately lift in training and in competition.

Many of the world's strongest athletes developed their formidable strength from weight training centered around the three powerlifts—the squat, the bench press, and the deadlift. These athletes include ice hockey players from the Soviet Union as well as track and field performers from Europe, Africa, and North America. In the short time that the powerlifts have been seriously practiced by athletes, they have earned a solid reputation as being among the most physically rewarding of exercises, and are without a doubt responsible for much of the increased strength, endurance, and agility displayed in today's sporting contests. Athletes have learned to exploit these lifts to improve physical development and increase overall body strength.

When training for powerlifting competition, never emphasize muscle strength at the expense of the style and performance of your powerlifting. In fact, when starting a powerlifting routine, the most sensible approach is to use lighter poundages that will allow you to perfect the proper form required for each lift (just as for the Olympic lifts). The following step-by-step instructions present the fundamentals of each powerlift so that you can achieve the proper lifting style to reach your full potential as a competitive lifter.

Illus. 93—Powerlifting requires more brute strength than Olympic lifting.

Safety Note: There is nothing inherently dangerous about power-lifting, but, as in almost any sport, potential dangers await the careless and thoughtless participant. Just as you would not risk diving off a high board without ever having dived before, do not attempt to squat or bench press a weight without full knowledge of your own strength. Furthermore, when planning to squat or bench press a weight that is reasonably heavy for you, ask for the assistance of other lifters in the gym to stand by, or "spot," for you. Usually for a heavy squat, one spotter on each end of the bar is needed. For a bench press, only one spotter is needed to stand behind the bar.

The Squat

Because the leg muscles are considered by many athletes as the core about which true body strength is built, the squat has been dubbed the "king of exercises." The squat concentrates almost entirely on the leg muscles and works them better than any other exercise. Specialists and strength coaches have noticed that concentrated exercise of the leg muscles is beneficial not only to the muscular system as a whole, but also to the respiratory system.

Top powerlifters commonly squat two-and-a-half to three times their bodyweights. Use a lifting belt (see pages 124–125) when squatting with moderately heavy and heavy poundages.

Object of the Squat

The squat is a deep knee bend done with a barbell across the shoulders at the back of the neck, followed by a return to the original erect position. During competition, the lifter "gets set" with the barbell across his back, and proceeds when the referee commands "down," or "squat." On completion, the referee will signal to remove the barbell.

Performance of the Squat

Place a loaded barbell horizontally in a rack at a height slightly lower than that of your shoulders. The squat rack may be a permanent fixture on the wall of a gym, or two portable vertical squat stands.

Position yourself beneath the barbell so that it lies across the back of your shoulders, and grasp the bar with an overhand grip, the thumbs wrapped around the bar (Illus. 94a). The width of your grip is a matter of comfort and, in time, you may alter your initial grip. The maximum grip-width, however, is limited to the inside collars of the bar, but not on the collars.

Try to place the bar a little below your neck (the lower the better). Most lifters find a comfortable, meaty area of the shoulders on which to rest it. Others find the bar uncomfortable in any position and wrap a towel around the bar to act as a cushion. The rules of competition allow padding to be placed around a bar, but it cannot be thicker than 2 inches (5 cm.) or wider than 12 inches (30 cm.).

Lift the bar up and off the rack by straightening your legs. Move a step or two forwards or backwards, depending on the arrangement of the rack (Illus. 94b). Establish your balance with your feet flat on the floor or mat. Position your feet so that your stance is slightly more than shoulder-width, and point your toes slightly outward. Actually, the wider your stance, the easier you will find the squatting movement, although not everyone has hip joints that allow a really wide stance. By no means stand with your feet closer together than shoulder-width. You would not be able to get your buttocks low enough when you squat.

Fix your eyes on a spot several feet above your head and keep them on that spot throughout the entire squatting movement.

Take a deep breath and hold it.

Illus. 94a—In preparation for the squat, find a comfortable region of the shoulders on which to rest the bar.

Illus. 94b—Be sure that you are well centered beneath the bar for good balance.

Begin squatting or lowering your body, exhaling slowly as you descend (Illus. 94c). During the descent, keep your back as erect as possible, by developing an arch in the region of the small of the back (Illus. 95a). And keep your head up and eyes fixed on that spot!

Stop descending when the tops of your thighs are slightly below parallel to the floor (Illus. 94d). Keep your back arched and erect (Illus. 95b). In the beginning, you will not be able to know if you are close to a parallel position. Have someone else (your spotter) observe your first attempts until you become accustomed to how the "parallel position" feels.

Do not squat much lower than parallel. Otherwise, unnecessary strain is placed on your kneecaps. A parallel (or slightly below parallel) squat is considered a *full* squat. (The ruling on exactly what constitutes a full

Illus. 94c—Begin to exhale as you begin your descent.

Illus. 94d—The movement must end with a full squat (see text).

Illus. 95a and b—You can have a slight arch in the small of the back, but otherwise your back should be straight. Do not squat lower than necessary.

squat varies according to jurisdiction. The current AAU ruling is that the tops of the thighs must be parallel to the floor. However, international rules state that an imaginary line between the knee and the hip must be parallel, thus making judging easier on men with bulging thigh muscles.)

Obviously, the ascent is the demanding part of the squat, not only on your legs and lower back, but on your form. In essence, the ascent is a retracing of the descending movement, with the emphasis placed on the strength of the legs and hips, and not of the lower back. Recovery from the full squat position should be performed with the driving force of your legs and hips, with your back erect and slightly arched, and with your head up. Continue to exhale gradually as you rise.

Some lifters find it helpful to cock their heads back as far as possible during the recovery. This helps them keep their backs erect and concentrates their attention in the legs and hips.

The lift is completed when you are erect and your knees are locked. Replace the bar on the rack.

Key Points of the Squat

● Keep your back arched, or as erect as possible, and the head up during both the descent and ascent.

● Inhale deeply before descending. Exhale during both the descent and ascent.

Special Notes for Competition

(a) After removing the bar from the rack, establishing your balance, and standing erect, you must wait for the referee's signal (a hand clap or a verbal command) before beginning the squat.

(b) Do not change the positions of your hands or move your feet during the squat.

(c) Do not shift the bar on your back while squatting.

(d) After completing the lift, do not replace the bar on the rack until the referee's signal.

The Bench Press

The bench press is responsible for outstanding chest and shoulder development among powerlifters. A good light- to medium-bodyweight powerlifter can usually bench press double his bodyweight. Many of the heavy lifters can handle 400 lbs. (180 kg.) effortlessly. However, you should start light, like all lifters did.

Object of the Bench Press

The bench press is an exercise performed by lowering a barbell from an extended-arm position while lying on a bench to touch the chest, and returning, or pressing, the bar to its original extended-arm position. During competition, the lifter lowers the bar at his convenience. The moment it touches the chest, the referee will command to "press," either with a verbal command or by a hand clap. Upon completion of the press, the referee signals to remove the barbell.

Performance of the Bench Press

Place a loaded barbell horizontally on a rack at one end of a specially equipped bench. Lie on the bench so that your forehead is approximately beneath the bar and your upper back is flat against the bench. Your feet should be flat on the floor (Illus. 96a).

Reach up and grasp the bar with an overhand grip, making sure that you wrap your thumbs around the bar. The width of your grip can be anywhere from slightly wider than shoulder-width up to a maximum of 2.65 feet (81 cm.) between the forefingers. Note that the wider your grip, the more of a role your chest muscles (pectorals) will play during the movement. The narrower your grip, the more the backs of your upper arms (triceps) will be used. You will assuredly establish your most comfortable grip after you have been "benching" for a while. It should be one that capitalizes on the use of the massive chest muscles.

Push the bar off the rack and hold it with extended arms approximately over the region of your shoulders (Illus. 96b). For safety purposes, have a spotter in back of the bench. You may prefer to have a spotter assist you in lifting the bar off the rack (called a "pick"), particularly when the poundages you select become heavy for you. Picks are allowed during competition.

Lower the bar to the chest, inhaling to expand your lungs and chest throughout the descent. Aim for the region of the nipples (Illus. 96c). Keep your body and feet motionless.

Lightly touch your chest (which is now filled and expanded) with the bar and pause for a split-second (Illus. 96d). Do not bounce the bar off your chest in an effort to begin raising it or let it rest deeply on your chest.

Illus. 96a—To begin the bench press, your position must be firm and steady.

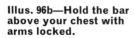

Illus. 96b—Hold the bar above your chest with arms locked.

Begin pressing the bar up, exhaling slowly as you do so, and concentrating on the force exerted by your pectorals, front deltoids (shoulders), and triceps. Push the bar in a path that retraces the descent. The bar should end over the region of your shoulders.

During the press, do *not* allow the bar to move forwards (towards your legs). Pushing the bar out and away from your shoulders will cause you to lose the "groove" that comfortably guides the bar from your chest back to the original starting position. Keep your upper back and hips firmly on the bench at all times and your feet planted solidly on the floor. Illus. 97 shows a lifter with bad form. His hips and feet are raised in a vain effort to press the bar. In competition this would disqualify the lift. You are, however, allowed a distinct arch in the small of your back (Illus. 96d).

The lift is completed when your arms are fully extended and your elbows are "locked." Replace the bar on the rack.

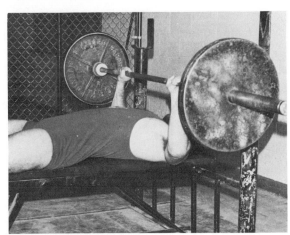

Illus. 96c—Inhale as you lower the bar to your chest.

Illus. 96d—An arch in the lower back is permissible. Touch the bar lightly to your chest.

Illus. 97—Note that this lifter's buttocks have come up off the bench and his feet are not flat on the floor. Not only is this poor form, but the lift would be disqualified in competition.

Key Points of the Bench Press

● Inhale while lowering the bar to your chest. Exhale while pressing it back up.
● Keep your upper back and hips on the bench, and your feet flat on the floor.
● Do not let the bar move forwards during the press from your chest.
● Use a spotter for safety!

Special Notes for Competition

(a) Do not change your body position after you have started the bench press.

(b) Do not bounce the bar off your chest. Wait for the referee's signal (usually a hand clap) after touching the bar to your chest before you begin the press.

(c) Do not press the bar unevenly. Keep it horizontal throughout the entire movement.

(d) After pressing the bar, wait for the referee's signal before replacing it on the rack.

(e) Do not touch any part of your body or the loaded barbell to the uprights (racks) on the bench.

The Deadlift

In the deadlift, each lifter accomplishes his or her maximum poundage. This is because the two largest muscle groups, the legs and the back are used throughout the movement. Some super-heavyweight lifters have deadlifted 800 lb. (360 kg.)! However, you need not be *that* ambitious. Start light and use a lifting belt for added support in your lower back.

Object of the Deadlift

Grasp a barbell lying horizontally on a platform with two hands and lift it up from the floor in one continuous motion until you have straightened to an erect position. During competition, the lifter must hold the barbell in the erect stance for about two seconds, until the referee signals to lower the bar.

Performance of the Deadlift

Place a barbell horizontally on a wooden platform or thick rubber mat. Approach the barbell so that your shins are directly behind the bar. Stand with your feet about shoulder-width or slightly wider, and with toes pointed slightly outward (Illus. 98a).

Grasp the bar with *one overhand and one underhand grip,* and with both hands on the outsides of the legs. Some lifters keep their legs outside the grip, and, rarely, a double overhand grip is used. Most lifters find maximum deadlifting strength with the stance and grip illustrated.

Establish a solid position with your feet and firm up your grip by squeezing the bar tightly. A firm, strong grip is critical for a successful heavy deadlift.

Look upward, drop your hips and buttocks down, and keep your back flat or with a slight arch in the small of the back (Illus. 99a). Inhale deeply.

Begin the upward movement by driving with your legs and hips, as if you were trying to press your feet into the platform using the bar as leverage (Illus. 98b). Exhale during the initial "driving" process as well as throughout the entire upward pull on the bar. This initial lifting of the

Illus. 98a—Get set for the deadlift with your feet shoulder-width or slightly farther apart.

Illus. 98b—Use one overhand and one underhand grip.

Illus. 98c—The final position must be erect with shoulders back and knees locked.

Illus. 99a and b—Remember to keep your head up and your back straight throughout the lift. Inhale deeply before you begin.

bar is concentrated in the leg and hip muscles. Keep your buttocks down and your back flat (Illus. 99b). Do not round out your back during the pull.

Continue to press with your legs, keeping your head up and your back flat, and exhale. As the bar is rising, keep it as close as possible to your legs. Keep the bar moving smoothly throughout. Do not jerk the bar in an effort to reach the erect position. When you are about halfway through

Illus. 99c and d—The upwards motion should involve all of the leg muscles. You should feel as though you were trying to drive your feet through the floor.

the movement, you will find that the strength required will shift from your legs to your middle and lower back muscles.

When near the erect position, drive your shoulders back and your hips forward (Illus. 98c). The lift is completed when your knees are locked and your shoulders are thrust back (Illus. 99d). Hold that position for about two seconds and then lower the bar to the platform. Keep your grip on the bar as you do so.

Key Points of the Deadlift

● Keep your back flat and drive with your legs. Do not put the burden on your back muscles. The deadlift should make maximum use of your leg strength.

● Keep your head up.

● Do not jerk the bar up with your arms at any time during the movement.

● Upon completion of the deadlift, thrust your shoulders back and lock your knees.

Special Notes for Competition

(a) Do not make a false start, or a false pull on the bar. Either will count as an official attempt.

(b) Do not stop the bar once it is in motion.

(c) Keep your feet motionless throughout the entire lift. Do not shift or raise your heels or toes.

(d) Do not lower the bar until the referee gives his signal (either vocal or a hand clap).

(e) Dropping the bar to the platform after completion of the deadlift can negate an otherwise good lift.

Training for Powerlifting

Perhaps the subject discussed most often among powerlifters is the training regimen. And rightly so, because success in competition depends in large measure on the preparations made during the weeks and months before a particular meet. Any lifter who is making super gains in strength between meets must be doing *something* right (the logic being, of course, that what works for that lifter will certainly work for me).

This conclusion is, unfortunately, not always the case. Much experimenting is required for any individual powerlifting training regimen. A scheme that has proven highly successful for one athlete may not work for others with different physical make-ups, life-styles, and (most significantly) body chemistries, which respond differently to otherwise similar situations. Where one person can do 10 sets of 5 reps with a moderately heavy barbell and make steady gains, a second lifter may burn himself out entirely when he attempts the same routine. Similarly, successful lifters who practice deadlifts twice a week may wrongly persuade a friend to do the same, not knowing that it may take a full week for his friend's back and leg muscles to recover between deadlift workouts.

It may sound as though there is no ideal power-training regime, but don't despair. The sensible approach is to start with a universal regimen, one that will get you well on your way to making substantial improvements. All aspiring powerlifters can initially follow this starting scheme identically, and only after several months of hard training will each lifter begin to deviate from this universal regime and experiment with variations.

As in training for Olympic lifting, you *must* keep a progress record that charts how you handle weights, reps, and sets of a certain lift, and the frequency of workouts per lift per week. There is a delicate balance between training and over-training in powerlifting, and you want to be sure to achieve a balance to remain on the track of continual progress.

Unlike Olympic training where assistance exercises are more important, an essential part of power training is performing the lifts themselves. Do not rely too heavily on supplementary exercises, although they are a necessary part of training. The only way to become proficient at the power-lifts is to do them!

However, you do not have to perform each of the three lifts at every workout. Powerlifts are very taxing and combined, they work every major muscle group of the body. You cannot expect your muscles to recover fully between workouts if they are tested during each workout. Keep an alternate three-day schedule, with one two-day rest period (for example, Monday, Wednesday, and Friday, with the weekends off).

Any powerlifting regimen should concentrate on squats and bench presses twice a week and the deadlift only once. Because of the intensity of a typical powerlifting workout, there is no way for your legs and chest to recover completely from *more* than two sessions of squatting and "benching" per week. Similarly, one solid workout a week at the deadlift, which places heavy emphasis on the legs and lower back, will be sufficient. Remember that your legs and back are well worked by squats the other days of the week, so don't worry about their getting stale.

Before your power regimen can get off the ground, you need to establish your approximate "best" at each lift (just as you do in Olympic-style training). You will always work on a percentage basis. The values in the regimen on pages 110–111 refer to the percentage of the maximum you are currently capable of lifting.

It is also important that during each workout you *gradually* work up to the most weight you plan to lift during that workout. Start with a "light" set and follow with progressively heavier sets until you reach your maximum poundage for the day. At that point, do the suggested number of sets and reps in the schedule.

Begin your workouts with 5 to 10 minutes of general warm-up and stretching exercises (see pages 76–79) to loosen the whole body. Follow this general warm-up with some specific movements to loosen the areas that your planned powerlifts will later work. For example, your general warm-up could include about 3 minutes of side-bends, jumping jacks, and some jogging in place. Specific warm-up exercises might consist of the following:

For the squat: Stretch the leg muscles and buttocks with about 10 deep knee bends, some lunging (Illus. 101), and toe-touches. Also stretch your lower body by stooping, pulling and bouncing lightly at the rack (Illus. 100).

For the bench press: Loosen your triceps and pectoral muscles with a few push-ups and parallel-bar dips.

For the deadlift: Prepare your legs and back with some deep knee bends, squatting deeply during some. Also do toe-touches and some lunging.

The suggested training regimen on page 110 specifies the number of sets and reps you should do before reaching your maximum *for that day* (indicated by "prep" for preparation). The maximum for the day is indicated by the percentage listed which is the percentage of your "best." The plus (+) signs included in the 100% mean that you should try to establish a new "best" at that time.

In addition to the powerlifts themselves, perform 2 or 3 supplementary exercises during each workout. Organize your assistance schedule so that you systematically work contiguous muscle groups. In this way, you can take advantage of blood already concentrated in a particular area. If you exercise your shoulders and the muscles in that area are congested with blood, the next logical exercise might be one for the chest muscles which are nearby, rather than for the legs which are quite distant from the shoulders. A solid one-hour workout is adequate for any powerlifter seeking substantial strength gains.

Do not hesitate to vary your supplementary-exercise scheme every few months. This will not only keep you physically fresh, but will help your mental outlook as well by breaking up and reviving what may have become a deep-rooted and boring routine. The sets and reps listed with the supplementary exercises spell out *all* the work you should do in one session, and the percentages refer to the maximum weight you should handle in the exercise.

This proposed regimen can be used to start anyone on his way to powerlifting competition. It is designed to test your maximum strength on a particular lift every third week. You do not peak on more than two lifts in any particular week or on two lifts on the same day.

Every three weeks you should go for a new "best," even if it is only 5 lb. (2.5 kg.) higher. When you post a new maximum, recalculate your percentages accordingly for the next three-week cycle.

Illus. 100 (right) and 101 (below)—As in Olympic lifting, it is imperative that you loosen up before powerlifting.

POWER TRAINING REGIMEN

MONDAY

Week I
Squat
prep.* — 2-3 sets; 5 reps
70% — 3-5 ; 5
Bench press
prep. — 2-3 sets; 5 reps
80% — 3-4 ; 5

Week II
Squat
prep. — 2-4 sets; 5 reps
85% — 3-5 ; 4-5
Bench press
prep. — 3-4 sets; 3-5 reps
90% — 3-5 ; 3-5

Week III
Squat
prep. — 4-5 sets; 3-5 reps
95-100+% — 5 ; 1-2
Bench press
prep. — 3-4 sets; 4-5 reps
85% — 3-4 ; 4-5

WEDNESDAY

Week I
Deadlift
prep. — 3-4 sets; 3-5 reps
80% — 3-5 ; 3-4

Week II
Deadlift
prep. — 4-5 sets; 3-5 reps
90-100+% — 5 ; 1-2

Week III
Deadlift
prep. — 2-3 sets; 4-5 reps
70% — 5 ; 4-5

FRIDAY

Week I
Squat
prep. — 2-4 sets; 5 reps
90% — 3-4 ; 3
Bench press
prep. — 2-3 sets; 5 reps
70% — 4-5 ; 5

Week II
Squat
prep. — 2-3 sets; 5 reps
75% — 3-5 ; 4-5
Brench press
prep. — 2-4 sets; 5 reps
75% — 4-5 ; 5

Week III
Squat
prep. — 2-4 sets; 5 reps
80% — 3-4 ; 3-5
Bench press
prep. — 4-5 sets; 3-5 reps
95-100+% — 5 ; 1-2

* Preparation sets for the weight to be used that day (which is indicated by the percentage of your "best").

Supplementary Exercises†

MONDAY		WEDNESDAY		FRIDAY	
Bent-over rowing	(4 sets; 5–8 reps) (70–85%)	Stiff-legged deadlifts	(3–5 sets; 3–5 reps) (60–90%)	Bent-over rowing	(4 sets; 5–8 reps) (70–85%)
Dips	(3–4 sets; 10 reps)	Presses	(3–5 sets; 3–5 reps) (70–90%)	Dips	(3–4 sets; 10 reps)
Leg extensions	(2–3 sets; 8–10 reps) (70–85%)	Hyper-extensions	(3–5 sets; 10–20 reps)	Leg curls	(2–3 sets; 8–10 reps) (70–85%)
Leg presses	(3–5 sets; 5–10 reps) (70–90%)	Front squats	(3–5 sets; 3–5 reps) (70–90%)	Leg presses	(3–5 sets; 5–10 reps) (70–90%)
Dumbbell bench presses	(3–4 sets; 5–10 reps) (70–90%)	Inclined bench presses	(3–5 sets; 3–5 reps) (70–90%)	Dumbbell bench presses	(3–4 sets; 5–10 reps) (70–90%)
Laterals	(3–4 sets; 5–10 reps) (70–80%)	Triceps extensions	(3–5 sets; 5–10 reps) (70–80%)	Laterals	(3–4 sets; 5–10 reps) (70–80%)

† Choose two or three exercises for each workout.

Once again, it must be stressed that *this is not a permanent regimen* but is designed to get you started in powerlifting. Some may find it valuable for making continuous gains for a year. Others may begin to deviate from it after a few months. (You may find that the three-week cycle is too short or that doing the deadlift only once a week is, after all, not frequent enough to make continual gains.)

Another feature of this scheme is that at the higher percentages, fewer reps are required. Development of strength in the powerlifts comes from doing sets of high poundages at low reps. Heavy "singles" (single reps) are essential for gaining strength and muscle bulk. Muscle size is directly related to the intensity of the exercise. Size increases are accompanied by increases in the number of capillaries in the muscles. And the greater the muscles, the better the powerlifting.

Supplementary Exercises for the Powerlifts

An axiom among powerlifters is that the only way to get good at the lifts is to do them. However, by adding some key supplementary lifts to your routine, you will be able to speed your progress. Accomplished powerlifting comes from working hard on the powerlifts and a select group of supplementary exercises.

In addition to the exercises suggested here, you may wish to refer back to the exercises presented on pages 25–52 and 82–90, and experiment with some of those in your training. For those supplementary lifts requiring a heavy barbell, perform sets of 3 to 5 reps; for non-barbell movements, do sets of up to 10 reps.

Exercises for the Squat

There is no question that squatting movements are the best exercises to improve the squat. If you have access to leg-extension and leg-press machines, take advantage of them to help in your leg development.

Front squats: For variation in squatting and for somewhat different activation of the leg muscles, you might try holding the bar at the front of your neck rather than in normal squat fashion across the rear of the shoulders (see page 26). To alleviate the strain on your wrists while doing front squats, rest the bar along the front of your shoulders on the "cushion" provided by the deltoids. Front squats will strengthen the muscles above the knee more thoroughly than back squats. In both cases, however, you will need a rack or squat stands on which to place the bar before and after the lift.

Leg extensions: Use a leg-extension machine (see page 28) to develop the quadriceps, the tops of the thighs. Be careful not to strain the kneecap region by attempting to raise too much weight.

Leg curls: Strength in the hamstrings, which form the rear of the thighs, is essential for good squatting. This is commonly a weak point because it's an area difficult to work directly. Do 5–10 reps of curls on a leg-extension machine (see pages 27–28) with a relatively light weight (50–70 lb. or 20–30 kg.).

Leg presses: Perhaps the supplementary exercise that best simulates the squat is the leg press (see page 27). In addition, when you work a leg-press machine, you can concentrate on pushing heavy weights without calling on the back muscles for assistance or worrying about the balance of the bar. Leg presses will greatly improve your recovery from the squat.

Exercises for the Bench Press

Improvement in the bench press is dependent on working the pectoral, deltoid, and triceps muscles. Almost any exercise that resembles the body movement of the actual bench press can be used as an excellent means of increasing power for this lift. Several exercises isolate the appropriate muscle groups.

Inclined bench presses: Isolate and develop the upper pectoral muscles by pressing weights while lying on an incline bench (Illus. 102). Depending on the layout of your gym, you may require assistants to hand you the bar while you are in the inclined position. A variation of this exercise is the

Illus. 102—Bench pressing on an incline is great for building the upper pectorals.

declined bench press (with your head lower than your chest), which adds strength to the lower pectorals.

Dumbbell bench presses: Assume the normal bench-press position but use dumbbells instead (see pages 36–37). Dumbbells let you lower the weight farther than when using a bar. As in the regular bench press, breathe in while lowering the weight. Also do dumbbell bench presses on incline and decline benches.

Dips: Stand between two parallel bars and hoist yourself until your feet hang loosely. Start with your arms straight, and lower yourself as far as possible (see page 50). Press back up. After you can do several sets of 10 with relative ease, tie weights around your waist to provide added resistance. This exercise works the triceps and the lower pectorals, particularly if you cross your legs and lean forward. The lower pectoral area is one that the bench press itself doesn't activate as well as dips, but building strength there will certainly contribute to further progress in your bench pressing.

Laterals: Pectoral development is greatly aided by laterals, which eliminate the use of the triceps and emphasize the use of the chest area (see pages 37–38). With dumbbells in hand, lie with your back down on a bench and extend your arms upward so that the dumbbells touch. Then, spread your arms open to lower the dumbbells to the side as far as possible. Then raise them. You can do laterals with your arms either straight or bent, depending on the weight you are using.

Presses: Build deltoid strength by pressing a barbell in either strict military fashion or from behind the neck (see pages 40–41). Do either variation using a standing or sitting position.

Triceps extensions: Isolate the triceps (which are greatly needed for the last half of the bench press) by sitting at the edge of a bench and holding one dumbbell behind your neck. Raise and lower the weight behind your head (keeping your elbows in a fixed position), inhaling while lowering (see page 49).

Exercises for the Deadlift

The supplementary exercises in this section emphasize lower-back development because the back muscles are all-important in deadlifting. That is not to say that the legs should be ignored, because they certainly play a major role in deadlifting, but the legs should be sufficiently prepared from doing squats and the supplementary exercises on pages 25–29.

Illus. 103—The deadlift requires a great deal of power in the back and legs.

Bent-over rowing: Perform a rowing motion with a barbell while bent over at the waist (Illus. 104), to exercise the lower back, the middle back, and triceps.

Illus. 104—In the position shown, simply raise and lower the barbell.

Stiff-legged deadlifts: Lifting a weight from the floor while keeping your legs stiff is a key exercise in developing the pivot area for the deadlift—the lower back (Illus. 105). Nothing isolates the lower-back region like stiff-legged deadlifts, a movement that is similar to hyperextensions. The greater weight used helps increase the muscle size and strength of that region.

Illus. 105—Deadlifting with straight legs isolates and develops the lower back.

Hyperextensions: Hyperextensions are a great way to develop back strength. Use either a special apparatus designed for this movement, or simply lay across a bench while someone holds your feet (see page 32). When you get proficient at hyperextensions and can do 20 or more reps with ease, add resistance by holding weights behind your neck.

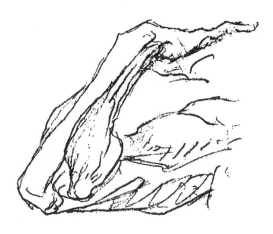

SECTION
V

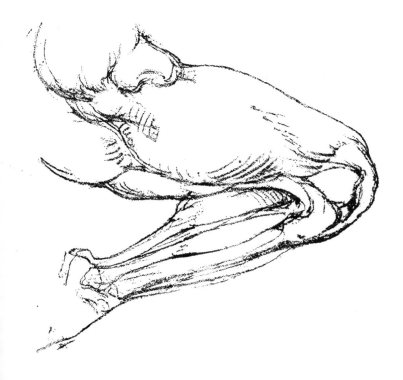

Entering a Competition

With your background knowledge of the fundamentals of competitive lifting and how to perform the competitive lifts and train for them, you are well on your way to getting involved in actual competition. Fortunately for newcomers, weightlifters are a unique group of athletes who welcome new competitors regardless of their level of muscular and athletic development. Discouraging a novice from competition is unheard of. Regular competitors know that you don't become good at this sport unless you compete, and they want to provide newcomers opportunities to participate and become good.

Weightlifting meets are generally held on Saturdays at YMCA's and athletic clubs, on college campuses, or in school gymnasiums. Usually, there are enough local contests to enable the novice lifter to participate in competition several times a year. If you begin to think in terms of regional contests, there should be enough to keep you in steady training.

Illus. 107—Your first competition will be a great help in correcting faults in form and technique.

To enter a meet sanctioned by the Amateur Athletic Union, it is essential to have an official AAU card. This must be obtained on an annual basis from one of the 58 local associations across the U.S. (the one closest to your home) at a minimal cost. To find the address of the association in your area, you can contact a Chamber of Commerce or the sports department of the local newspaper. Or, if those approaches fail, you can obtain a list of the 58 associations from the AAU headquarters at 3400 West 86th Street, Indianapolis, Indiana 46268.

For residents of Canada, England, and Australia, the sports organizations which are equivalent to the AAU and necessary to contact about weightlifting regulations are:

Canadian Weightlifting Federation
333 River Road
Ottawa, Ontario, Canada

Australian Amateur Weightlifting Federation
P.O. Box 114K
Melbourne, Victoria 3001, Australia

British Amateur Weightlifting Association
3 Iffley Turn
Oxford, England

In addition, residents of *any* country who desire information on competition can contact the international offices for Olympic lifting and powerlifting.

For Olympic lifting:
International Weightlifting Secretary
1442 Budapest PF, Hungary

And for powerlifting:
International Powerlifting Federation General Secretary
P.O. Box 6024
Arlington, Texas 76011 USA

Who's Qualified to Compete?

There are very few official regulations for eligibility. Practically everyone can compete. The only exception is the minimum age for powerlifting (16 years). Otherwise, weightlifting is wide open to those of all ages, all bodyweights, and both sexes. In the United States, some Amateur Athletic Union-sanctioned meets are held exclusively for Juniors or for Seniors. (A Junior is a lifter who is under 20 years of age. On a lifter's 20th birthday, he or she is considered to be a Senior.) In some cases, a meet may be limited to lifters from a certain geographic region, to members of a club, university, or athletic league. Most meets, however, are "open" in this regard.

Contrary to what may seem like common sense, there is really no need for an upper age limit for competitive weightlifting. Most individuals who have spent time in their youth working out with weights, or who have recently undergone some conditioning, can continue to lift and train with as much weight and as frequently as they desire. There is no reason in the world why a healthy 50-year-old man should not train to bench press 300 lb. (135 kg.) if he has the musculature and health to do so. Moreover, competitive weightlifters often do not reach their peak in strength and ability until they are in their thirties. While many amateur athletes in other sports are finished by the time they reach their late twenties, most weightlifters will have not yet reached their prime.

The number of women weightlifting is definitely on the increase, but they do not as yet represent a great percentage of those in competition. Certainly there are not yet enough to hold contests exclusively for

Illus. 108 and 109—Age and sex are not barriers to lifters. Anyone can compete.

women, which means, of course, that women who are strongly interested, intrepid, and well-trained step right in to do battle against the men.

The Equipment

The barbells and weights used during competition are unlike the moderately-priced weight sets that you may have been using for weight training at home (see page 17).

The foundation of official weightlifting equipment is a 1.1-inch (28-mm.) thick, finely-tooled chrome-vanadium bar, whose ends are covered with revolving sleeves where the weight-plates are attached. This Olympic bar, as it is called, is 7 feet (2.1 metres) in length and 45 lb. (20 kg.) in weight. To accommodate a sturdy and firm grip, competition bars have a rather

Illus. 110 and 111—The official Olympic bar.

deep knurl encircling the portion where lifters place their hands. The plates, or discs, used in combination with these competition bars most commonly come in weights of $2\frac{1}{2}$, 5, 10, 25, 35, and 45 lb. or $1\frac{1}{4}$, $2\frac{1}{2}$, 5, 10, 15, 20, and 25 kg. Each plate is clearly marked as to its weight. Bars are loaded with the largest disc on the inside, with progressively smaller discs towards the outside (Illus. 110–111). Special locking collars are placed over the ends, or sleeves, of the bar to retain the discs snugly in place. The total weight of the barbell and collars is 25 kg.

The gym you choose to work out at may have wooden platforms or thick rubber mats of various sizes on the floor to protect it from damage by the weights. When it comes to an actual contest, the lifting must be carried out on a wooden platform that measures four metres on each side. This platform must be sturdy enough to withstand the unintentional dropping of heavy barbells when lifts are missed.

Your attire when you work out is optional, but competitions require you to wear the proper costume. This is normally referred to as a lifting suit, which is a one-piece combination of trunks and a tank top. A tee-shirt can be worn beneath the lifting suit provided that it does not have long sleeves or a collar. An athletic supporter, or jock strap, is part of the attire for men. A lifter's shoes or boots can have heels, but they cannot be thicker than $1\frac{5}{8}$ inches (4 cm.). Special quality lifting shoes that have ankle supports, arch supports, and heels can be purchased.

An important piece of equipment used by nearly all lifters is a lifting belt (Illus. 112–113). Wider than a normal belt, the lifting belt protects the back and midsection when lifting heavy poundages. More important, however, is that it gives you a greater sense of security, which in turn enables you to lift at your full capacity. Belts wider than $3\frac{7}{8}$ inches (10 cm.)

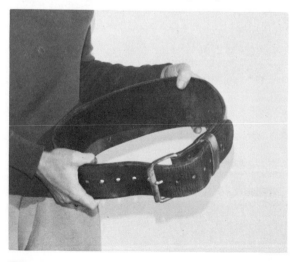

Illus. 112—The lifting belt.

Illus. 113—Properly worn, the lifting belt lends support and protection to the lower back.

are forbidden in competition. A good leather lifting belt can be purchased through a mail-order house or from a sporting goods shop.

An optional part of a lifter's equipment is gauze bandage. Some lifters, in an effort to give extra support to their knees or wrists, or to prevent recurrences of old injuries, prefer to wrap these areas with gauze or medical crepe. In competitions, bandages cannot exceed a metre in length for the wrists and 2 metres for the knees. There are also regulations for the width of bandages: 3 inches (8 cm.) for the wrists, $1\frac{1}{2}$ inches (4 cm.) for knees during Olympic competitions, and 3 inches (8 cm.) for knees during powerlifting. Bandages are not permitted around the hands or the body.

Bodyweight Classes

Olympic lifting began with nine weight classes. It did not originally have a 220-lb. (100-kg.) class until after the 1976 Olympic Games, when

Illus. 114—Gauze bandage is a permissible part of the lifter's attire (see text).

Illus. 115—The complete attire for a competitive lifter, including lifting suit and lifting belt.

the International Weightlifting Federation voted to add a 100-kg. level to the competition.

Powerlifting also originated with only nine bodyweight classes, from a 123-lb. (56-kg.) class to the class for men over 242 lb. (110 kg.). The sport did not have a flyweight class like Olympic lifting, because it was thought no one under 114 lb. (52 kg.) would ever be interested in or physically qualified for a strength sport like powerlifting. Contrary to these expectations, the popularity of powerlifting grew so rapidly that there was soon a definite need to instate a flyweight class to accommodate the substantial number of small men and women who were in fact interested in competing and who qualified for a lower weight.

Today, in either type of weightlifting, Olympic or power, the 10 bodyweight classes are:

	up to 52 kilograms	*up to 114½ pounds*
Flyweight	up to 52 kilograms	up to 114½ pounds
Bantamweight	56	123½
Featherweight	60	132¼
Lightweight	67.5	148¾
Middleweight	75	165¼
Light heavyweight	82.5	181¾
Middle heavyweight	90	198¼
Heavyweight	100	220¼
Light super-heavyweight	110	242¼
Super-heavyweight	*over* 110	*over* 242¼

The weighing-in at a contest is to be done by each lifter in the nude, and within one hour before the contest. Each competitor is allowed only one weigh-in, unless he or she falls marginally between two weight classes. If this is the case, the lifter is allowed another chance to make a specific class by weighing-in a second time within the allotted hour. As should be obvious, a lifter cannot compete in more than one weight category during a meet.

Scoring

Becoming a winner in either an Olympic lifting or powerlifting contest is a matter of totaling the most weight. That is, the individual who lifts the greatest total weight *in each bodyweight class* as determined by the sum of the snatch and the clean and jerk (in Olympic lifting), or by the sum of the squat, bench press, and deadlift (in powerlifting), is declared the winner. Achieving the best, or highest, weight in only one lift does not earn the competitor the winner's mantle—it is the total weight of the two or three lifts that counts. To provide all competitors with ample opportunity to perform their best, each individual is given three attempts to perform each lift.

Note: In some powerlifting meets, three attempts are not permitted for each lift. Instead the lifter is allowed only two attempts on two of the powerlifts and three attempts on one lift of his choice. This is referred to as the "wild-card" system and it is used as a means of expediting meets. Whether or not the wild-card system is used at a particular meet is usually decided beforehand by the meet director or at the weigh-in by a majority vote from the competitors.

Obviously it is not fair to compare the total weight accomplished by a super-heavyweight to that lifted by a middleweight competitor. Individual accomplishments are compared only within a particular weight class, just as in any other bodyweight-structured sport, like boxing or wrestling. Within each weight class, three places are recognized—first, second, and third. In the event of a tie, where two competitors in one bodyweight class achieve identical totals, the winner is the individual having the lower bodyweight within that weight class. For example, if two competitors lift the highest total weight of 500 lb. (226.5 kg.) in the light heavyweight class of an Olympic meet, and they weigh 175 lb. (80 kg.) and 170 lb. (77 kg.) respectively, the 170-lb. man will be declared the winner. Second place in that class would go to the heavier competitor.

In weightlifting competitions, lifters can compete as individuals, as team members (a team may represent a club or a particular gym), or as both. Team scoring is conducted separately from the individual scoring and points are awarded for each member of a team who places first, second, or third. In most contests, first place is allotted 5 points, second place is allotted 3 points, and third place is valued at only 1 point, although in some events points are given to the top 10 finishers. The sum determines team placements. Of course, some teams will have more members than others and they are obviously at an advantage, but if the members of a smaller team place first or second as individuals, they may as a group outscore other larger teams.

Lifting Order

The order of lifting during a contest (whether Olympic or powerlifting) is determined by the weight on the bar. Each lifter performs when the bar is at a weight he wants to attempt. When a lifter's name is called by the announcer, he has two minutes before beginning his lift.

Illus. 116—Spotters are allowed even in competition. *Always* have spotters on hand when performing a heavy lift.

After a successful first attempt, the lifter's second attempt must be at a weight at least 10 lb. (or 5 kg. in international meets) heavier. If that second attempt is also successful, the increase in weight for the third and final attempt must be at least 5 lb. (or $2\frac{1}{2}$ kg. in international competition).

An individual who fails to succeed in one lift in the competition (say the snatch in Olympic lifting, or the bench press in a powerlifting meet) after the allotted three attempts is disqualified from the contest. In lifting circles, that is referred to as "bombing out."

Usually lifters will begin, or "open," with a weight they are confident of lifting successfully (a poundage that they have lifted easily during training sessions), since success on that first lift will secure a position in the competition. Their second and third attempts can then be used to approach or achieve their "maximum" poundage, or the weight they feel will make a total needed to win that particular contest.

The weight of the barbell continues to increase as the contest progresses, and a competitor cannot request that the weight of the barbell be decreased. You must at all times keep track of the increasing weight on the bar and inform a referee, director, or expeditor about 10 minutes before each lift of the poundages you plan to attempt. If your first or second attempt at lifting a certain weight is unsuccessful, the bar will be held at that weight to allow you another chance at it if you wish. Otherwise, the bar "goes up."

After a successful lift, the waiting time for your next attempt will depend on how many other competitors will be trying to lift poundages lighter than what you have specified as your next lift.

Judging

During competition, some attempts at lifting are obviously unsuccessful. But sometimes a competitor will appear (and believe himself) to have completed a lift successfully, and then be told that the lift was not good because of certain flaws in form. For example, a bench presser who slightly raises his buttocks from the bench to assist in pressing the barbell from his chest will be ruled as having performed a "bad" lift. But who decides?

As in any other competitive sport, there are officials for weightlifting. They decide what is fair and within the rules. Three referees position themselves around the lifting platform, one in front and one on each side (Illus. 118). Each referee casts a vote on the lift and indicates his judgment by switching on either a white or red light after each lift. A total of two or

Illus. 117—The judges would disallow this lift because the lifter is touching the platform with his hand.

Illus. 118—The arrangement of judges around the platform. Note the light box (to the left of the lifter) with which they signal their verdict.

three white lights indicates a successful lift. Two or three red lights signify a "bad" lift.

For certain lifts, the chief referee at the front of the platform initiates the lift with a command. For instance, when a powerlifter gets into position for a squat, he must wait until the chief referee commands "squat" to begin. Similarly, the chief referee will signal "down" when a lift like the snatch is successfully completed. To be sure that the lifter hears and understands the command, most referees use the sound of a hand clap followed by the verbal command.

There are many ways in which each lift can be rated unsuccessful, even though the lifter may appear to have done well. These have been pointed out in earlier chapters that described the lifts in detail.

Competitors who place first, second, and third in their weight classes are awarded trophies for their achievements. At many meets, a "best lifter" award is given to the individual who totals the most weight with respect to his bodyweight. These awards are sometimes given to two individuals: one for the five lightest weight classes, and a second for the best lifter in the five heaviest weight classes.

In addition, lifters can earn a series of patches that testify to their strength and ability. These patches signify the total weight lifted in a weight class during either an Olympic or power meet, and are ranked: Class IV, Class III, Class II, Class I, Master, and Elite. It's the Master and Elite patches that competitors make a point of displaying.

Table 1. "Totals" required to earn AAU classification patches for Olympic lifting

Ratings	Bodyweight (pounds*) classes									
Total pounds* lifted	114	123	132	148	165	181	198	220	242	242+
International Elite	485	524	562	622	684	733	777	799	827	865
Elite	441	474	513	568	717	667	706	722	750	783
Master	402	436	463	518	568	612	640	667	684	717
Class I	364	397	425	469	513	557	584	606	623	550
Class II	320	347	369	408	452	485	513	524	546	568
Class III	264	286	303	341	369	402	425	436	451	468
Class IV	226	243	259	292	320	348	358	375	386	402

*Multiply the number of pounds by 0.45 to obtain kilograms

Table 2. "Totals" required to earn AAU classification patches for powerlifting

Ratings		Bodyweight (pounds*) classes											
		114	123	132	148	165	181	198	220	242	242+
Elite		1080	1160	1240	1360	1480	1605	1710	1825	1905	2100
Master		1000	1075	1150	1250	1375	1485	1575	1650	1750	1900
Class I	Total pounds* lifted	890	960	1030	1110	1230	1325	1400	1490	1590	1700
Class II		780	850	920	990	1070	1150	1230	1320	1400	1500
Class III		680	740	800	860	930	1000	1080	1155	1225	1325
Class IV		575	635	695	750	810	870	950	1010	1070	1170

*Multiply the number of pounds by 0.45 to obtain kilograms

Records are made to be broken in weightlifting. Although setting a new national record in a particular lift and weight class can still be done, it is more reasonable for novice lifters to set their sights on a local record for a particular gym, YMCA, university, or city. Records are kept not only for the individual lifts themselves, but for the highest totals as well. It is possible, then, to establish three new records for each weight class in Olympic-style lifting, and four new records for each weight class in power-lifting.

What's Your Choice—Olympic or Power?

At some point in your training, you will want to choose which of the two types of competitive weightlifting you wish to train for.

An important factor in your decision will be the type of action you expect from a sport, mainly as a participant, but as a spectator as well. If you like agile, fast movements accompanied by techniques that must be performed to perfection, then Olympic lifting is the competition for you. Agility, speed, and finesse are the keys to success in this event. The Olympic lifter is an athlete who appreciates fine and well-developed control over the movement of the body. Indeed, a proper performance of the Olympic lifts is quite artistic. On the other hand, you may be fascinated with solid, formidable strength and massive musculature and care less about speed and finesse. You then have reason to pursue powerlifting for competition, where the emphasis is on power.

Before you decide, try to attend at least one meet of each type of lifting so that you are completely familiar with what is expected of the participants and how each type of meet is conducted. Then examine your present musculature and reflect on your experience and success in previous athletic efforts. What do you hope to achieve physically from your preparations for competition? Perhaps native strength has always been your prime asset, and you already have a good foundation upon which to build and train as a powerlifter. On the other hand, you may have excellent speed and co-ordination, which has helped you excel on the basketball or tennis court, and therefore Olympic lifting would be the choice for you. Do not overlook any physical handicaps you may suffer. If your knees have given you problems in the past, you may not want to specialize in squatting and powerlifting. If you have had surgery on your shoulders, you may be apprehensive about snatching, or perhaps you no longer have the flexibility required for that movement.

Some outside factors that you must weigh in your decision are the time available for training as well as the availability of equipment and partners.

You may find it necessary to devote an extra hour or more a week if you train for Olympic lifting, because you must work longer on the techniques involved in Olympic lifting. Do not take this as an ironclad rule, for you may find that your body trains more quickly for Olympic lifting. If time is a critical factor in your weekly schedule, you will want to establish the relative times necessary for training for each type of lifting.

The equipment you will find available is also something to consider, but it should not be a major factor in your final decision, and in most cases is not an insurmountable problem. It may only require shopping around for the proper gymnasium or purchasing some equipment for your home gymnasium.

Illus. 119—The agility required for Olympic lifting makes this a graceful sport to watch . . .

Illus. 120—. . . while powerlifting demands solid, well-developed musculature. The choice is yours.

Finally, you may find more interest among your friends for one type of lifting over the other. Working with partners is very helpful and if you know a number of people already in training, you may want to join them in their choice. The same is true when it comes to coaching. If you know someone who can offer advice and help you develop your techniques, you may make your decision by taking advantage of that person's knowledge of either Olympic or powerlifting.

Establishing a Training Schedule for Competition

Aside from actually doing the lifts, the most important part of becoming a good competitive weightlifter is establishing a proper training schedule. On pages 80–81 and 110–111, specific training regimens were given for both Olympic lifting and powerlifting. Here the emphasis will be on the *dos* and *don'ts* of preparing for an actual meet.

The key parts of a training schedule are time, frequency, and intensity. When you work out depends entirely on your personal schedule and the time of day when you feel most ambitious and energetic. About the only strict rule is to leave adequate time for food to be digested before working out. Usually, this means that you would wait two hours after eating a major meal before lifting weights. Otherwise, your workouts can take place at any time—right after rising, or before going to bed. It is wise to time your workouts to that part of the day when your energy level is at its peak, which varies from person to person.

How often should one train when preparing for competition? The answer is simple and straightforward: no more than three times a week and no less than two times a week (three times a week is normal for competitive lifters). After a vigorous workout, your body needs at least 48 hours to recuperate fully, and, in fact, that may not even be enough time. It is imperative that your body has a solid 72-hour (three-day) rest once a week, so schedule your workouts for Mondays, Wednesdays, and Fridays, and leave the weekends for the three-day rest. Don't be misled by statements that some lifters work out as much as six days a week. These are probably bodybuilders not training for competitive weightlifting, and they have probably been working very hard with weights for 5 or 10 years.

An intense workout need not go longer than one hour. More than that, and you will have reached a point of diminishing returns. The length of the workout is a touchy subject among weightlifters because it is so common to equate more with better. In weightlifting, this relationship just does not hold. Too much training means over-training. Work too long and you no longer build up strength, but may start to tear it down.

Stick to a three-times-a-week workout schedule and avoid spending more than an hour on each training session (assuming that you work out nearly continuously throughout that hour). You will be tempted to do one more set, or one more new exercise than you had planned, but learn to resist those temptations. It does not take long to become a good lifter with respectable strength, so don't try to cram two years of training into one.

Finally, proper diet and nutrition are critical for your training. These are topics discussed at length on pages 151–155, but the essential points cannot be overstressed:

● Never skip breakfast. Eat something substantial like granola or eggs.

● Avoid high-calorie foods, like sweet rolls and french fries.

● Eat fresh fruit each day and several helpings of leafy vegetables.

● Drink several glasses of water each day. Also drink milk in copious quantities (to save money, try non-fat dry milk).

● Eat ample amounts of complete proteins.

● Vary your meals to be sure that you are including all possible nutrients, and consider taking vitamin supplements, particularly vitamin C, the B-complex vitamins, and possibly vitamin E.

Illus. 121—Proper mental attitude is essential for weightlifting. A good lifter is confident and determined.

Mental Attitude

For most people, the greatest part of the day is taken up by jobs, family life, or schoolwork and weightlifting is likely to play a relatively small role. Sometimes, lifters enter the gymnasium for a scheduled workout bringing along problems related to their careers or their personal lives. Such problems quickly take their toll and distract from the quality of the workout. Mental attitude can be as important in weightlifting as speed, technique, or even strength, and unfortunately, a poor attitude (however temporary) can stifle motivation and interfere with concentration. Outside problems can make the weight you used two days earlier seem twice as heavy today.

Keep a good attitude—approach each workout as though it was going to be your best, and leave your problems outside the gym. Of course, this is easier said than done, and requires a little self-discipline. But if you are already hooked on weightlifting, you may find it easier to train yourself mentally to dissociate personal problems from the physical experiences of a workout. If you have made weightlifting a normal part of your daily life, then you have achieved a certain degree of self-discipline. Strengthen your will further, and you will arrive at a point where outside pressures have little influence on your performance in the weight room. It is entirely up to you to develop that mental discipline.

There is one outside influence that can help alleviate mental burdens, and that is working with a partner. During each workout you can act as mutual supports, since you will soon come to expect a certain level of performance from each other. Friends can shake you out of the doldrums and inspire (or shame) you to put out your best for that day.

Of course there are other problems that occur in the gym. Sometimes you may begin your session with a clear mind, and find that your lifting isn't going as well as expected. Usually this is due either to over-training or to fatigue. Over-training was discussed in detail on page 137, and fatigue is above all a temporary condition. Do not let one bad workout affect your future progress. Get plenty of rest, and come back to the gym refreshed, ready to take up where you left off two sessions ago.

Preparing for a Meet

For your first weightlifting meet, mental and physical preparation are clearly the key factors involved. You want to work so that both peak on the morning of the event. Before that morning, however, there are a few miscellaneous, although necessary, items that you must take care of if you are going to participate.

Every meet requires you to submit an entry form which can be obtained from the meet director. Check to see that you have fulfilled any special qualifications (AAU membership, for instance), and mail your entry form to the proper person before the registration deadline. Most meets require a small entry fee, which can increase if you do not preregister but wait to sign up on the day of the meet.

When travelling to a meet, be sure to allow yourself enough time to arrive at the location. Take into account possible difficulties in finding the exact building and allow for possible transportation problems. On the other hand, do not arrive so early that you remain idle for a long time. If you start to worry about how well you will perform and how strong the competition will be, you can easily be drained of the nervous energy you will be depending on later in the day.

Take along items like a second shirt, shoelaces, enough wraps to keep warm in the lifting arena, and some high-protein snacks and juices to get you through the day. A frantic search for any of these items during competition could easily disrupt your concentration.

Illus. 122—Above all, a lifter must have great concentration to marshal the energy and power needed for a lift.

Mental Preparation

Mental preparation and conditioning is one aspect of sports competition earning more concern and attention each year. Professional teams in the U.S., as well as the Czechoslovakian national ski team employ psychologists. Norwegian universities offer academic degrees in sports psychology, and Austrian ski jumpers can attend an institute for will-power training. Experts in sports psychology have shown that mental well-being has a great deal to do with physical performance in a meet or game.

At the simplest level, we know that people perform better physically when they are frightened into action, triggering a flow of adrenaline throughout the body which enables them to overcome physical obstacles that would normally be insuperable. But this is an example of a momentary "psyching-up" which is of little use to the athlete. What he needs is long-term preparation that begins well before a contest and combines dedication, motivation, concentration, and self-confidence.

Dedication is perhaps not a quality that one can learn. It may manifest itself in a simple way (by not missing a workout even though a friend is over for the day), or it may involve great sacrifice of time and money. The secret is to have clear, honest, and tangible goals towards which you are working.

Motivation is the ordering of goals, and so is difficult to divorce from dedication. What are your priorities? Do you want to enter a meet merely for the fun of competing and with no concern for where you place, or are

140

you willing to work hard enough to earn a shelf of trophies? Do you want to set a personal record, or better public ones? You are the only one who can establish what is important to you. The higher you set your personal sights, the greater will be your motivation.

Learning to concentrate is learning to direct all your ability, energy, and attention towards one purpose—lifting that barbell. You must be able to shut out distractions and limit your whole sense of being to yourself and the barbell. Some coaches have their lifters periodically train in an intentionally distracting or disturbing environment in order to develop a mental toughness. This can come in handy, because there are occasions in a meet where unexpected events can disrupt your concentration. Unexpected developments, like a protested lift or the setting of a new record, can cause delays which might throw you off-stride. If you can marshal and concentrate your energies in difficult circumstances, you will be less likely to leave your best lifting performance in the training room.

Self-confidence is an exceedingly important characteristic that is essential to performing your best in a meet. To put it simply, think highly of yourself. There is no room for pessimism in weightlifting. Convince yourself that there is no way you can fail in the lifts you will attempt. *Know* you can do it! One psychological approach that will help you achieve a positive self-image is to visualize yourself successfully performing the lift so that success is well-planted in your mind. Almost all of us are capable of doing more than what we think we can, and it usually takes self-confidence to bring out that potential.

This brings us to a final point about mental preparation for a meet. What weight do you choose for your first attempt at each lift in your first competition? This will be one of your most critical decisions and is perhaps the most important aspect of competition.

The answer to that question is especially simple: *start with a weight that is easy for you to lift.* Select a weight you have successfully lifted many times before during training. You need the confidence that comes with successfully completing your first attempt. Missing that first attempt can be shattering! Never let pride influence your selection or feel embarrassed about selecting a relatively light weight for your first attempt. As a beginner, your prime concern should be gaining the experience of competition. Don't worry about beating other lifters who have been competing for years. This is a learning experience, and is not the time to be concerned about winning, or even placing. Remember, too, that you are not now lifting in training but are in fact being judged by three referees. That pressure and the unfamiliar surroundings can influence your performance. So allow for these unexperienced pressures and be sensible about the contest poundages you select.

For your second attempt, up the bar only the minimum increase of 10 lb. (5 kg.) for Olympic lifts, and from 10 to 30 lb. (5 to 15 kg.) for powerlifts, depending on the particular lift. At this time in your lifting career, there is no need to make wild jumps from one attempt to the next. Again, it's a matter of establishing good feelings about yourself, which will assuredly come if you are successful in all, or nearly all, of your lifts during your first meets. This second-attempt poundage should certainly be below your best in training.

Finally, on your third and last attempt, choose a weight equal or almost equal to the best you have accomplished in training.

Physical Preparation

To get physically in shape for that first meet, you must train steadily and intensely up to a week before the meet. Two weeks prior to the meet, you should work up to your limit poundages. During the week of the meet (when you do not want to tax your body or over-train), stay limbered up and keep your muscles accustomed to a substantial but not overwhelming load. Polish your style and form by practicing enough reps and sets.

Many experienced lifters schedule their training on an eight-week cycle before a particular contest. For the first two weeks of the eight-week period they go light and emphasize form in order to prevent peaking prematurely. During the third and fourth weeks, they still concentrate on form, but with heavier poundages. By the fifth and sixth weeks, they are ready to attempt the starting poundages they will select for the contest. In the seventh week, they may try their maximum in each lift. The last week is reserved for perfecting speed and form, and to iron out any small flaws. They do not engage in any heavy lifting.

Assuming that the meet is on a Saturday (as most are), your workout for the last week should be moderately heavy on Monday, then moderate to light on Wednesday. On Thursday you should just loosen up with a few sets of the competitive lifts and some selected accessory lifts. Do nothing on Friday. If you are going to a meet far from your home, you might be wise to travel on Friday. In any case, do not work out on the day before a meet. You want to be well rested that morning.

Many times a lifter is slightly over a bodyweight classification limit and into a weight class they prefer not to be in. If that is the case, watch your water and food intake carefully for 24 to 48 hours before the weigh-in. Usually it is water weight that can unexpectedly land you in a higher weight class.

When you get backstage, or in the pre-meet warm-up room, do about 15 to 20 minutes of stretching movements to loosen up your muscles. Start

Illus. 123—The week before a meet, workouts should not be as intensive as usual.

about 30 to 40 minutes before the estimated time of your first lift. Keep some sweat clothes on to maintain the warmth you build up and have a rubbing treatment on hand for added muscle warmth.

After that light workout, begin working on the lift you will perform first. But go easy with your tempo. Don't expend too much energy in the training room. You need to conserve that explosive energy for the competition itself. Time your warm-up sets so that you can get about five or six sets in before your lifting time comes up, leaving about three or four minutes rest between the sets. At first, estimating the starting time may be difficult because you do not have a feel for the approximate waiting times involved. This depends largely on how many lifts will be made before you and the weight of the first attempt.

Your warm-up lifts should reach poundages 20 to 40 lb. (10 to 20 kg.) under the weight of your first attempt. Do no more than two reps with the lighter weights and only one rep when you are near your starting poundage.

Your last warm-up should come about 5 minutes before your attempt. If you find that the wait is longer than you had counted on, do one-rep sets of 75 to 80 per cent every 4 or 5 minutes to keep loose. You do not even have to complete the lift, and can drop the bar right after the clean or the initial pull. Another technique used by lifters to remain warm while waiting is massage. Have a fellow lifter, coach, or adviser massage your major muscle groups in a circular motion. This will bring blood to the activated areas.

Illus. 124a-f—Get warm
and loose before a
competition and
maintain this condition
throughout the meet.

Illus. 124a

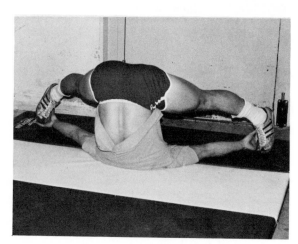

Illus. 124b

Illus. 124c

Illus. 124d

Illus. 124e

Illus. 124f

Between lifts, keep warm! Put on sweat clothes and stay loose. Move around so that you do not get stale, tight, or cold (this can happen in as short a time as 5 minutes). If the wait is long, do another warm-up with about 80 per cent of the weight you plan to attempt next. Again, you need not perform a complete lift. Stop the lift halfway through. The idea is to stay warm and ready.

After a few hours, you may become aware of your appetite. Don't hesitate to eat or drink, but keep it to a minimum. Eat a protein food, like peanuts or a granola bar, and do not try to eat hard-to-digest foods like hamburgers, milkshakes, or french fries. Drink water or fruit juices, but don't drink so much that you bloat your stomach and lose your concentration.

Illus. 125—A weightlifting meet is a great place for lifters to learn by watching other lifters.

After the Meet

One of the best learning experiences for your competitive lifting career will have been your first meet. Each beginning lifter should use that meet as a proving ground to check on his lifting progress.

Unless you are an unusually talented individual, you probably did not place all that well in your first competition, but do not let that discourage you. Your primary reasons for competing were to check the quality of your training regimen to find out which aspects of your lifting you need to polish, and to get a better gauge of your ability and a realistic appraisal of your personal goals.

Most major faults become quite obvious during a contest, and you will now want to work diligently to correct them before they become ingrained habits. Determine what your weak and strong points were and use them to re-evaluate both your training sessions and your next competition. Did you keep proper form, balance, and speed throughout the contest lifts as you practiced in training? Had you prepared enough, both mentally and physically or did you over-train?

Break any noticeably bad habits now! Ask others to coach you if you are trying to correct obvious problems with technique. Faults manifest themselves more readily in competition than in training because of the pressure of the competition. One important reason for entering as many meets as possible is to diminish the pressure of competition so that you can concentrate fully on your performance of the lifts.

You should also ask yourself some specific questions about your strategy and physical condition:

Did you make the proper bodyweight class? Did you choose the proper starting weights and then increase the weight of the bar in reasonable percentage increments? Was your initial selection for each lift appropriate? Did you allow yourself enough time to warm up before each lift and with weights in the correct proportion to the poundages you used during competition?

It is possible that you found the contest environment intimidating. Were you uncomfortable in the new and strange surroundings? Did the other lifters intimidate you or did the different environment affect your style? If any of these possibilities was the case, consider training in another gym once in a while so that you become accustomed to foreign surroundings and the feel of different lifting equipment, platforms, and people.

Remember to think positively about your first weightlifting meet, whatever the outcome. Learn as much from it about yourself as you possibly can. Enter as many contests as you can fit into your schedule. Improvement in competitive weightlifting is directly related not only to a solid training routine, good diet and rest, but also to the amount of actual experience you have on the lifting platform.

Illus. 126—Winning your first trophy is bound to be a rewarding and gratifying experience.

APPENDIX

Appendix

Diet and Weightlifting

Good weightlifters know not only about proper form and training techniques, but they have a thorough understanding of nutrition as well. How one's body improves in strength and overall development is directly related to how well it is nourished. You are, after all, a product of what you eat and a good diet will greatly help your training performance and your attitude towards it.

Protein

Protein is the most important concern in a weightlifter's diet. This is not to say that you should neglect other nutrients (carbohydrates, fats, minerals, and vitamins), but protein is singled out because ample amounts of it are essential to build strength and muscle.

The most abundant component of your body, aside from water, is protein, making up about half the dry weight of your body. One third of that protein is present in your muscles, allowing them to contract and hold fluid, giving them firmness. Structurally, proteins are made of amino acids, which are compounds formed from the elements carbon, hydrogen, oxygen, and nitrogen. Twenty-one amino acids are commonly found in body and food proteins, and your body has the ability to chemically change some of these into others as needed. There are 8 amino acids (known as the *essential* amino acids) that your body cannot produce, however, and these must be taken directly from the food you eat. As a weightlifter, you must eat in order to provide your body with enough of the essential amino acids to construct new body and muscle tissue. In order to increase muscle size and strength, you must consume ample amounts of protein each day. Protein is not a major source of the energy needed for weightlifting. Rather, it is a nutrient that is needed for muscle development.

Almost any animal product (meat, poultry, fish, eggs, and the milk products) are excellent sources of protein and contain what are called *complete*, or high-quality protein. This means that these foods have proteins that are of high biologic value and are composed of at least the eight essential amino acids, or chemical building stones, in the proportions needed for body development and maintenance.

Vegetable protein, with the exception of soybean, is normally not as high in quality as those of the animal products. Also, the percentage of protein in vegetables is much lower than in meats. Vegetable proteins can still be greatly beneficial, however. When two or more of these incomplete proteins are consumed, they complement each other, so that the body can utilize the amino acids consumed in combination. Soybeans are the one vegetable that has protein of quality comparable to that of animal products. Even when eaten alone, they are an excellent, low-cost source of body-building protein.

The amount of protein needed each day varies according to one's bodyweight. Protein values of various foods can be determined from tables in nutrition books, and the rule of thumb is to consume 0.8 grams of protein for every kilogram of bodyweight. In other words, a person weighing 165 lb. (75 kg.) should eat a minimum of 60 grams of protein daily. This recommended value is, however, probably too low for an active weightlifter. A minimum of one gram of protein per kilogram of bodyweight is more desirable for individuals concerned about muscle development.

Carbohydrates

Carbohydrates meet the immediate energy needs of the body and are found largely as starches and sugars in grains, vegetables, fruit, and the so-called "junk foods." Unused carbohydrates are stored in the liver (as glycogen) or converted to fat and stored as adipose tissue—something none of us need. Weightlifters should obtain carbohydrates for energy from vegetables, fruits, cereals, and dairy products, or from foods that provide other forms of quality nutrition. Keep the quantity of refined-sugar products, such as pastries and candies, to a minimum.

Fats

Like carbohydrates, the fats, or lipids, are a source of energy. Unfortunately, because of the association people immediately draw between fats and overweight problems, there is an unfounded tendency to fear this nutrient. Weightlifters should know that fats are the most concentrated form of energy in foods, yielding more than twice the energy per gram as carbohydrates and proteins.

The major sources of fats are vegetable oils, animal fats, cheeses, egg yolks, and nuts. When consumed, fats are deposited under the skin to insulate the body and remain as a major source of reserve energy. Of course, when one begins to get overweight, their fat stores far exceed what they need as energy in reserve. Take the same stance towards them as you do for carbohydrates, remembering that too much of either will lead to overweight problems.

Minerals

In addition to protein and the energy-supplying nutrients, competitive weightlifters should also have a knowledge of the minerals present in foods and the role certain minerals play in the body. Muscle contraction is a complicated process involving not only the intake of muscle-building protein and the presence of enzymes, but a contribution from minerals as well.

Weightlifters need to be familiar with calcium, phosphorous, sodium, potassium, magnesium, chlorine, sulfur, and iron and be aware of which foods supply each mineral.

Calcium is by far the most abundant mineral in our bodies, and is thought by scientists to play an important part in muscle contraction. (Potassium, sodium, and magnesium are also thought to play a role in these chemical reactions.) Moreover, calcium is believed to assist tired muscles in recovering and to delay muscle fatigue. The best sources of calcium are milk and milk products. Three glasses of milk are usually adequate to meet your daily requirements.

Phosphorous is necessary for strong bones and teeth and helps metabolize carbohydrates and fats. Diets are rarely found to be deficient in phosphorous, but a lack can cause weakness, bone pain, and the loss of calcium from bones. Phosphorous is present in fish, poultry, organ meats, milk, and whole grains.

Potassium, found in small amounts in almost all foods (especially bananas), helps regulate the body's water balance and functions in nerve and muscle action. A deficiency of potassium can lead to nausea and muscle weakness.

Sodium also regulates body water, and comes into play in muscle contraction and in maintaining nerve irritability. Salt is the major food source for sodium.

Magnesium, found in leafy green vegetables, works with some of the enzymes needed for carbohydrate metabolism and energy release.

Chlorine aids in the formation of gastric juices and in the absorption of vitamin B-12 and iron. Moderate amounts of salt will provide enough chlorine to fulfill the body's needs.

Sulfur is a significant part of the nails and hair, and it aids in the detoxification of certain chemical reactions within the body. Because sulfur forms part of some proteins, a protein-rich diet precludes a sulfur deficiency. You can obtain sulfur specifically from eggs, milk, and cheese.

Iron is exceedingly important in the process that carries oxygen to the cells and muscle tissues. The best food sources for iron are meats (liver in particular), egg yolks, leafy green vegetables, and dried fruits like raisins and prunes.

Vitamins

Vitamins are not essential to our bodies as muscle-building and energy-producing substances, but they are necessary in the metabolism of other nutrients and in maintaining a general physical well-being. A diet that is deficient in one or more vitamins does not necessarily cause serious illness, but it will certainly hamper good, overall health and vitality. If you suspect that you are not getting large enough quantities of a certain vitamin, don't hesitate to take vitamin supplements in the form of pills or tablets. Multiple-vitamin supplements often provide enough of these nutrients for weightlifters. Individually, we will only discuss vitamins D and E.

Vitamin D aids in absorbing calcium from the digestive tract to use in building bones. This is the only vitamin that the body can synthesize (with the help of sunlight). The other major source of Vitamin D is commercial milk that has been enriched.

Vitamin E is still a controversial compound, especially in the athletic community. Many athletes and scientists claim that it can maximize energy output, endurance, and performance, as well as prolong cell life. Major sources for Vitamin E are unrefined vegetable oils and cereal products, especially wheat germ and eggs.

Protein Supplements

Protein supplements are powders and liquids that are produced for weightlifters and bodybuilders concerned about muscle mass, strength, health, and stamina. They can be purchased at any health-food store and supply protein in concentrated forms to guarantee that enough muscle-building nutrients are taken each day.

Are these supplements really necessary for good weightlifting? Probably not. Your body can only utilize so much protein per day, and any excess is deaminized by the liver and used as carbohydrate or expelled. If you consume enough meat and milk products, you can be sure of having eaten enough protein and other nutrients for your weightlifting program. You may, however, wish to experiment with these supplements to decide about their benefits for yourself. Just be prepared to pay a premium price for protein in these concentrated forms.

Illus. 127

Index